# SACRED PATHS
AND
# MUDDY PLACES

# SACRED PATHS

AND

# MUDDY PLACES

REDISCOVERING SPIRIT
IN NATURE

## Stephen Altschuler

STILLPOINT PUBLISHING

# STILLPOINT PUBLISHING

Building a society that honors The Earth,
Humanity, and The Sacred in All Life.

For a free catalog or ordering information, write
Stillpoint Publishing, Box 640, Walpole, NH 03608, USA

1-800-847-4014 TOLL-FREE (Continental US, except NH)
1-603-756-9281 (Foreign and NH)

This book is manufactured in the United States of America.
Cover and text design by Karen Savary

Published by Stillpoint Publishing, Box 640
Meetinghouse Road, Walpole, NH 03608

Library of Congress Catalog Card Number: 92-062690

Altschuler, Stephen
Sacred Paths and Muddy Places

ISBN 0-913299-92-8

1   3   5   7   9   8   6   4   2

This book is printed on acid-free recycled paper
to save trees and preserve Earth's ecology.

This book is dedicated to Jean Maxwell (1900–1992),
a fellow walker, writer, thinker, and lover of nature.
She was a good friend and a bright light whose epitaph
should read, as she often said, "I hope you have as much
fun in life as I did." BON VOYAGE, Jean, and much love.
May we meet again to walk and watch and wonder
by the creekside in the garden.

# CONTENTS

# FOREWORD

This is a book about discoveries and the searching that leads to those discoveries. From simple foraging in the forests to profound explorations of the human spirit, it is the account of one man's odyssey in search of himself.

The initial expedition—a four-year sojourn in the birch woods of New Hampshire—leads to "important discoveries": an orange salamander, purple crocuses, Zen riddles, a fly with "Buddha courage," an ingenious beaver, and the silence of the forest. The experience forces deeper introspection. "Living things in the woods live whole lifetimes—in a moment," Stephen Altschuler discovers. "Moments are born, live, and then pass away, leaving the seed of a new moment."

After four years in the woods and a brief stint as a wanderer across borders both American and European, Stephen makes an abrupt change. His quest leads to California and the "polar opposite of life in the New Hampshire woods." Unnerved by the urban wilderness of Berkeley, the author discovers walking as the link to earth and to the sacred paths, the holy ground, the power spots. The country is found in the city, and the soul is found in the man.

From then on, the landscape becomes secondary to the inner surroundings. Whether wandering through woods, meadows, or city streets, Stephen finds the act of walking to be a metaphor for discovery, perspective, challenge, and triumph. While one is walking, as the author discovers, the human voice within one's self resounds with new fidelity.

This, then, is the record of changes in one man and his ongoing journey to All That Is. The road to self-discovery is always a footpath. Each of us must come to his or her own terms with the world, which is resplendent with sacred paths and muddy places.

Bradford W. Ketchum, Jr.
Editor, *The Walking Magazine*
Boston, Massachusetts

# ACKNOWLEDGMENTS

No published book is ever the product of one human being. It is a collaboration of often remarkable people and spiritual forces.

Deep thanks to publisher Meredith Young-Sowers and president Errol Sowers, who extended their faith and confidence; managing editor Charmaine Wellington, who offered great skill, humor, direction, and support; senior editor Dorothy Seymour, who gave valuable assistance; the rest of the Stillpoint staff, particularly Karin Bell, who said, "Yes, send in the proposal"; and to Hal Morris, publisher of Western Tanager Press, for allowing use of the following essays (all revised for this book) from my first two Bay Area books:

"The Hi-Line," "Spring," "Sacred Paths," "Walking Together," "Town Cats" (formerly "Berkeley Cats"), "Rain Walking," "Wildness," "Birds," "Flowers," "The Hi-Line Revisited," "Urban Wildlife," "Creek Walking," "Matters of Life and Death," "Mud Walking," "Coyote" (which first appeared in the *East Bay Express*), and "Falling Free" (which first appeared in *The San Francisco Chronicle*). In addition, "Ant Wars" was originally published in the *East Bay Express*, and another version of "To Leap Like a Tiger While Sitting" first came out in *East West Journal*. Many of the essays in the first part of the book aired originally on WSLE-FM in Peterborough, New Hampshire, as part of a weekly series I wrote called "Backwoods Cabin."

Great appreciation to the following friends for their love, support, and friendship as I wrote this book: Patrick Tribble, Gregg Levoy, Jean Maxwell, Bob Bartel, Terry Ojure, Sarah Greenberg, Bernice Moore, and Dorlie Fong. Thanks, too, to New England friends: Ferris Urbanowski, Al Jenks, Charlie Fisher, the Brummers, and Betty Ann Chase for their companionship and support in the face of garden-eating woodchucks and wild winters. I'm grateful also to Millie Alvarez, Genie Kaiser, and all the members and staff at Towne House Creative Living Center in Oakland, California.

I bow deeply to my teachers: Sasaki Roshi, Alan Watts, Krishnamurti, Orion, Zen Master Seung Sung, Joseph Goldstein, Thich Nhat Hanh, the Dalai Lama, and Ajahn Sumedho.

Finally, thanks to my mother, late father, and the rest of my family for their love, laughter, and support.

# ONE

## LIVING
## IN THE
## COUNTRY

A few months after I moved out of the city to a small cabin in the woods, my car was vandalized on Christmas Eve during a heavy snowstorm. Instead of gnashing my teeth or getting depressed, I chose to see this supposed calamity as a message from universal forces that wanted me on foot for a while. So I left the car where it was, and as the winter progressed it became a very interesting ramp for snowmobiles. Sometimes one man's Diaspora becomes another's Disneyland.

Through the rest of that winter and three more seasons to follow, I got around on skis and foot—quite well, actually—and for the first time began to notice things I had previously taken for granted, things I had not considered important enough to look at or hear. Like Henry Thoreau striding carefree along the banks of Walden Pond, or John Muir hiking to a Sierra peak, then climbing a pine tree to celebrate the wind, I found my turbid senses clearing. I began noticing and appreciating what was around me . . . like a cat on the roof of a porch, a creek just off the road, a column of chimney smoke, the groaning sound ice makes on a lake, a crocus peeking through the surface of the ground, a salamander discovered on the trail.

I began to discover a world full of sensory richness, perceived formerly only with senses dull as a neglected kitchen knife from run-around city living. Speed had inured me to think of the destination at the expense of everything in between. As a consequence, my mind raced as well, anticipating more than experiencing the moment at hand. And with only a finite number of moments available in this lifetime, I found I had missed most of them.

Now you might say, so what? What's so important about living each moment, anyway? The answer lies in the effects I enjoyed from slowing down: less anxiety, more peacefulness, being clearer in thought and deeper in breath. Life sparkled with more joy, interest, and appreciation, as if some part was returned—a part that, missing but unnoticed, made the whole feel unsettled, off-centered, incomplete. And all this from being literally back on my feet again.

Awareness catalyzed the return of that part of my life—an active way of seeing and living in the universe, of actually dancing with the universe. By slowing down to a walk, I entered for the first time into a true relationship with my environment. By opening inner doors I found that outer vistas became more accessible. And by paying attention to the outer world in deeper ways I discovered that my inner world became more available, richer, and more understandable, though not always peaceful.

The essays in this book reflect those changing inner and outer landscapes. They are personal but also universal. The period starting in Spring of 1977 describes the trials of a city man moved to a small cabin deep in the woods, about a mile and a half from my nearest neighbor. I sought a simpler life, so I sold or gave away most of my possessions, particularly the electric ones like photo enlarger, hair dryer, stereo, and TV, keeping only those items that I saw as important on practical, emotional, and spiritual levels, like hand tools, my old-friend guitar, and a few books like *Walden, Zen Mind, Beginner's Mind,* and *Webster's New Collegiate Dictionary.*

*STEPHEN ALTSCHULER*

I paid my last utility and phone bills and resolved to take more control over the basics of living—heat, water, light, food—as well as the vicissitudes of my own mind. I sought a place to write, not about other people's lives and experiences, as I had as a magazine and newspaper journalist, but about my own experiences—a more personal kind of journalism more integrated with my emotional and spiritual life. That kind of writing needed space, inside and out. It needed time as well, and in the city, with its emphasis on a material world that kept breaking down or getting in the way or being jammed, there never seemed to be enough time.

I was an early baby-boomer who had survived a six-year marriage consummated at twenty-four with a former college best-friend whom I seemed to love at the time, at least for the first three years. My main occupation then, in addition to part-time journalism, involved social work mostly in state prisons helping men cope with prison life by concentrating on their inner response to that Kafka-esque environment.

My own inner response to the prison, which helped stir up old fears about life-threatening situations, was to incur, rather suddenly, a severe phobia that, as I reflect on it now, approached a schizophrenic break, but one that I managed to control, barely, through sheer force of will . . . and by remembering the tranquil-izer in my pocket in case things really got out of hand. Working in the prison, with my increasingly unbearable agoraphobia, along with my confining marriage, which the phobia didn't help, made me the Age of Anxiety manifest.

My nemesis anxiety, and a growing discontentment with a legal and penal system totally bankrupt and hopeless, got me to quit the prison, and then my marriage, which felt like a large, dense bog—nothing dramatic, nothing bombastic, just a quagmire, which had me wondering if the next step would be quicksand. Shortly after we divorced I wrote in my journal, "At thirty I've managed to achieve a honed state of neurosis, a mutually-agreed-upon divorce, a three-room flat in Boston, and staying alive."

After the marriage ended I got the proverbial (for the mid-seventies) master's degree in counseling, worked a year with severely troubled adolescents, then left after my own anxiety level hit a flashpoint that said, like New Hampshire's license plates, "Live Free or Die" (plates that were manufactured, by the way, by prisoners in the state's penitentiary!). I then made the move to the woods. After seven years the phobic reaction had eased considerably. But I needed time alone, a lot of time alone—to heal, to reflect on the course my life was taking and where I wanted it to go.

The cabin held me in its bosom, as I sat by day at a huge nineteen-twenties rolltop desk that almost filled the entire room (I'd rescued the monolith from my father's office in Philadelphia years before), lying down or meditating in the sleeping loft when the sun went down. For a while I muddled about in a sort of trance, and when it rained, which was often that fall, I sat motionless, listening to the tinsel beat on the building's metal roof.

The first time I saw the cabin the winter before I moved in— the cabin that was to become such a healing space—I remember thinking, "I couldn't possibly live here." Its one room (actually two— the outhouse was connected to the cabin with an inside door leading to it) and sleeping loft measured eleven feet wide, twelve feet deep, and about sixteen feet high. The cabin boasted no utilities, and it sat braced at the base of the north side (that's the cold side!) of Barrett Mountain in New Ipswich, New Hampshire. The rent was $25.00 per month.

This was no idyllic writer's colony, where all the creature comforts were in place, freeing the muse to romp in the tall grass. No, with water to fetch, wood to haul and cut, and food to store and prepare without gas or electricity, earning a living became much different from punching in and getting a paycheck every two weeks. Earning a living and living became synonymous, with payday being every day, more or less.

I soon discovered, though, that the physical demands of the

woods life paled compared to the emotional, that living alone and the absolute silence and raging storms that shook both the house and my confidence were far more formidable than coping with no kerosene or lack of indoor plumbing. And it began to occur to me that living in such a way was pushing on internal limits. So, as the days moved on—much more slowly, it seemed, than in the city—a learning commenced, not a learning of facts and figures or dates and data but a learning born of life experience alone, a learning inherent in living and honed by the quality of awareness I could bring to the ordinary aspects of everyday life, a life that revolved much less around acquiring and using material possessions, a life closer to its bare root essentials.

At first my new life was confusing. I had not been trained to learn in this way. In the past I'd simply try to go around pain or discomfort or avoid it until I got what I wanted with as little trouble as possible. At the cabin, though, this strategy often failed.

On the one hand, time seemed slower in the woods, but on the other, circumstances could make the need to respond immediate. The woods and the nature that filled it became a teacher, at times uncompromising, at times stern, but always wise, giving me exactly what I needed. And I came eventually to trust its messages and ways.

On the day I moved in I sat back and reflected, with pen in hand, on this revolution in living I'd embarked upon: "I am now sitting still in my cabin, looking out the greenhouse 'bay' window up the slope of Barrett Mountain. Am listening to a mouse exploring my belongings. So defined, its patter against the crystal silence of the outside air. I am filled with awe, a sense of wonder . . . and fear too.

"I feel like staying up all night and listening to the void—the Tao. I am crying—for the journey before me. I am crying for joy—the silence."

I continued crying, not always for joy, and laughing and sitting quietly and listening, listening to the steady pulse of nature and a heart that was beginning to trust itself and reconnect with a spirit momentarily dormant but deeply and inherently alive.

Four years later, after leaving the woods—a departure precipitated mostly by those legendary long, hard New England winters—I traveled, literally in search of sun, finally settling in Northern California. Though not as sunny as Easterners think, California was still considerably warmer than New Hampshire, so I could easily be outdoors year-round. I continued writing, publishing two books about urban walks, reflective essays, and local Bay Area history, and again worked in social service on a part-time basis, this time with the elderly in nursing homes. As with prisons, nursing homes have their own walls, and my work there, which still continues today, was meant to bridge those walls with good-natured contact.

But it was still the city and, after a second marriage, which began lovingly and simply, life soon became more complex. My answer to the complexity was to look for natural places within walking distance where my mind could settle and clear, where I could return to the richness of the senses and the essentials of the spirit that I experienced in that small country cabin. I've begun each chapter about my adventures with an attempt to show what was going on in my tumultuous mind as I sought balance in the natural, quiet places I'd discovered in the city.

The places mentioned in this book may or may not have meaning for you, but the inner "places" within those places will be familiar. They are the "places" of fear, joy, sadness, laughter, love, anger, pain, camaraderie, doubt, faith, hope, despair, and trust. I have grown from opening the senses that led to these internal places— an opening, an end, that used walking as its means—and by doing so have, I hope, affected the health of this planet in a positive way, if only by consciously not harming it very much.

The quality of awareness and attention I applied to daily life yielded the other means of growth, including the awareness of not being aware—a realization that broadens the universe's cosmic smile.

This quality of consciousness, this active awareness, is the ultimate destination I sought. It had the potential of bringing great joy to the planet and to oneself.

So you can't really lose when practicing awareness. Awareness means suspending judgement for a moment (which, by the way, doesn't mean you have to give up cursing the chair leg after stubbing your toe!), then seeing, feeling, experiencing what this condition in front of you is all about. Life then becomes alive and organic, forever changing, driven less by memory than by the immediacy of the moment. No need to figure out the moment intellectually or the way you want to respond to it.

For through awareness you are living fully, and by stepping back and seeing yourself be aware, you find that the judging mind fades, allowing the emergence of love, compassion, and enduring faith. You can handle anything that arises and can let it go to face the next moment, tasting its treasures in whatever form.

The universe, which some might call God or nature or All That Is, is there to be seen and appreciated for what it is, even its painful manifestations, and being seen, it will offer all its abundance. Our inner universe wants, too, to be felt in all its richness, regardless whether we were abused or coddled, encouraged or negated, wealthy or poor. It—all of it—just wants to be acknowledged and embraced. When we yield to that need, then we love ourselves: we love Earth. We love ourselves: we love animals. We love ourselves: we love people. We love ourselves: we love the sacred paths and muddy places that no vandal can take away from us. We might even love the vandals, like the ones who trashed my car that Christmas Eve, for opening whole new worlds we'd never before considered.

Sacred Paths and Muddy Places affirms the interconnection of the external world to our internal world, and through awareness offers a way of healing both the planet and ourselves. We needn't set out to "improve" the environment—or ourselves—but only to open our eyes, ears, nose, tongue, touch, and heart. Improvement, taking action, as in the raising of a child, will then arise out of the wisdom such attention spawns.

Then the universe breathes a little easier as it feels the love, and our lives become more alive with one discovery after another.

STEPHEN ALTSCHULER

# DISCOVERY

Living in the city before coming to the woods, I spent most of my time, as I think about it now, planning or preparing for some future event or reward. The present moment was a blur, an inconvenient delay in the rush to get somewhere. So when I first moved to the cabin in the spring of 1977 my level of awareness compared to city levels. I spent a great deal of time preparing for the coming winter, which I'd been warned about. In the first weeks, consequently, many of the wonders of the woods passed me by. Although I lived at the base of this lovely (albeit, at about 1,700 feet, little) mountain, I was like the fellow whose home is in the next town over from the Taj Mahal and hadn't seen it yet. I kept saying, "I've gotta climb that mountain. Maybe tomorrow."

But this day, finally, I cleared away everything. I could find no more excuses. And the hike and subsequent discovery I made became *pivotal events that set the tone, pace, and spirit for the months and years ahead of living in the woods.*

With Barrett Mountain beckoning me daily just by being there, any further delay in climbing it would have led to personal and eventually—once word got out—societal embarrassment. A backwoodsman, even one born and bred in the city, had a reputation to uphold.

So off I went, as intrepid as any Everest explorer, up this mountain that would seem like a hill to a Coloradan. Upward I trekked, letting the mountain decide which way to go. Bramble, thistle, tangles of dead branches, fallen and now rotted leaves tugged and snared my legs as I loped through it all like a deer in deep snow. A fairly stout staff, picked up in the early going, furnished a faithful prop and got me out of some knee-deep spots. The going was slow, and several times I thought about turning back, with remarks like, "Boy, it seems to be getting pretty dark," and "I think I forgot to close my door." Actually, the time neared two o'clock on a May afternoon, and I had closed my door obsessively so mosquitoes wouldn't get in.

But I continued and finally came to a stone wall, which I thought was remarkable, since someone built it halfway up the mountain. It formed a trail, so I followed it, but after a few hundred steps I discovered something that was to change my attitude for the rest of the hike and for days and weeks to come. There in full view, directly in my path on decaying leaves and tiny twigs, crawled an animal I hadn't seen in twenty years. And after eight years of living in New England I had decided it did not exist in this region. It was a plodding, almost comical, four-legged critter that had filled many childhood summers with good times and excitement, with the thrill

*STEPHEN ALTSCHULER*

of the search and the compassion and caring for those found sick or wounded—like the one with gangrene on its tail that I found, and nursed, at summer camp in the Poconos years before.

That day, halfway up Barrett Mountain, I discovered an ordinary orange salamander—ordinary to those experienced in the lore of the northern woods but absolutely unique and enchanting to a man who lived most of his life in cities and, unless he made a special trip to the Poconos, had long ago given up the hope of holding a salamander again.

It seemed as if important discoveries always happened that way: when I stopped seeking what I wanted, I found it. The word for it was *serendipity*, the gift of finding valuable or agreeable things not sought for. I yelled out when I found that salamander, yelled out in joy as I did when I was a boy. "I've got one! Over here!" And my friends would come running, hoping that they too would catch one over in my greener—or is it orangier ?—salamander pastures.

I felt light and buoyant after that discovery and marveled at my rendezvous with this long-lost creature. Somehow, finding the salamander affirmed that everything would be okay, that I would find my Golden Fleece if only I wouldn't look so hard. Somehow, this discovery took one more rock from my shoulders. Somehow, it laid everything out—the joy, the peace, the hopes, the dreams, the struggling, the pain, arranged in a simple harmony, waiting to be discovered by a discoverer who was not out to discover anything.

I picked up the little creature and looked it close in the eye as it sat motionless on my palm. This being just lived in this world with all the skill it knew, lived with the one trait that I had been trying for years to regain after knowing it early in life: trust. Aside from its color, which blended into the terrain, the slow, lumbering salamander had no other defense. It just trusted, or intuited, or just knew instinctively that this monster who had picked it up would handle it with care and not harm it. Trust was the lowest common denominator of its tenuous life—the assumption that other larger beings would let it alone if found. For the most part, the trust it extended matched the trust it received, and it went on surviving and living its life. I returned the salamander gently to the trail. Could I learn from this supposedly lower life form?

The rest of the hike was a high time. I breezed to the summit, tromped over blueberry bushes and giant glacier-strewn rocks to gaze at the serene Monadnock valley below and the mountains beyond. At that moment the hike stopped being a hike separate from my life in the cabin below. It was all the same—one discovery after another: one hope, one dream, one love, found, savored, and taken in. One wildflower spotted. A smell recognized. Soil felt. A joke laughed at. All the same. Out there like that salamander.

When I returned to the cabin, I sat at my desk and looked out the window up the slope of the mountain, thinking that it now looked more like a friendly old neighbor than something to be avoided. I'd come a long way, not in time or distance but in spirit and awareness, from the city where moments and their contents often went unnoticed in the mindless fog. That mountain and its serendipitous salamander now occupied a part of that trusting niche in my mind, along with all those other things and events and living beings that I could conjure up at a moment's notice and through which I could re-live the discovery.

# TO LEAP LIKE A
# TIGER WHILE
# SITTING

Before coming to the woods I had been exposed to Zen meditation from taped lectures of the late philosopher and Zen popularizer
Alan Watts. I had heard about a particular Zen retreat from a new
friend who lived on the other side of the mountain. She praised the
teacher, a Korean Zen Master, and his disciplined form, suggesting it
would help my sporadic, and inadequately directed, meditation practice.

Zen practice works on developing concentration, honing awareness,
and emptying the mind of the filtrate of too much thought. The silence
of the woods was at first as deafening as the noise of the city, so I
knew I needed mental surgery of some kind. With that attitude, along
with a vague, anomalous idea of getting spiritually enlightened I left the
woods for a weekend in the city to swallow a dose of Zen.

But like the proverbial cure that was worse than the ailment, a weekend of Zen made the woods life seem like a tea party. It was torture, although the training I received in letting go of each moment and accepting each life event as it is served me well in dealing with the only absolute truth I knew of: things changed.

I knew from Watts that Zen dealt with core issues of life and death, but moving to the woods, alone, brought those issues to the front lines of my life. I thought of death a great deal. Infinity. Scary stuff that living in the cabin highlighted in bas relief. Sadness, too, welling up from depths whose source I didn't know. But, on some visceral level, I knew that instead of backing off from such fear and sadness, as I might have in the past, I needed to go into the maw of those emotions. Zen sounded awesome and arduous enough to be the right vehicle.

Shortly after moving to the cabin my new friend Ferris told me about a three-day Zen retreat at the Cambridge Zen Center near Boston. I had been practicing Zen on my own for about a year before coming to the country but had avoided its austere group involvement. So, although I could stay in my woodland home and dutifully do Zen meditation (called *zazen*) for forty-five minutes or so, my spiritual practice still needed some kind of validity from Zen friends on the other side of the mountain who were starting to think that I was doing my morning sitting in the prone position, snoring.

Only after I said "Okay, Ferris, sign me up" did she tell me the name of this retreat, or *sesshin*: *Yong Maeng Jong Jin*, which in Korean means "to leap like a tiger while sitting."

"What are you getting me into, Ferris?"

"Relax. You'll be fine. Besides, the food is great."

So with the trust of that aforementioned salamander I went back to the noisy, cantankerous city for a weekend with Zen and my own mind and body. The center itself, located in a blue-collar neighborhood, was no Taj Mahal, and dormitory living had its down sides, but I welcomed the break for a bit from the outhouse and hauling water.

After getting settled, twenty-five of us filed into the meditation room to hear Zen Master Seung Sung, or Soen-sa-nim, as he was called, give the opening Dharma talk (*Dharma* is translated roughly as "all the laws of nature"). He was a small, somewhat oval-shaped monk, made even more so by his loosely fitted robe. His face beamed friendliness, seemingly immune to the wrinkles of twentieth-century Western life, and was quite literally glowing with what I guessed to be enlightenment and love.

"All mind same," he began, in broken but intelligible English. "Your mind, my mind, same. Original mind all same. Original mind, don't-know-mind. When we keep don't-know-mind, your mind, my mind same."

I had read his book, *Dropping Ashes on the Buddha*, and was familiar with his teachings. I came holstered with questions: Why must I sit *zazen* every day? Why do I get scared when my legs start hurting during long sittings? How can I overcome my fear of death? Isn't attaining enlightenment, the ripest Zen fruit, anathema to the Heart Sutra (literally, the heart of Zen teachings), which says there's nothing to be and nothing to attain? Isn't it enough that I'm living in the woods in a simple way, not harming the earth? Why must I go through these apparently contrived austerities? Why? What? How? Many questions for Zen city hall.

But others, too, had urgent questions; and judging from their quickness in asking, they must have been waiting at the gates for a long time. "I don't seem to be getting anywhere with my practice," droned one rather gaunt female disciple. "I have a lot of bad sittings."

Soen-sa-nim: "Bad sittings. Good sittings. Put it down. Put it down and go straight ahead. Keep don't-know-mind, and no 'bad,' no 'good.' Thinking. Thinking. Always thinking. Original mind is don't-know-mind. Then can't have bad sitting or good sitting. Just sitting. Just like this. Who are you?"

"I . . . er . . . ah . . . I don't know."

"No, I mean who *are* you? Your name." (Laughter.)

"Oh? Mary James."

"Who were you before you were born?"

"I . . . er . . . ah . . . I . . . I don't know."

(Smiling.) "Don't know. Good. Don't know. Only keep this don't-know-mind."

So much for any of my questions. He probably wouldn't know the answers, anyway. Besides, I kind of liked the pain in my legs. And death: big deal. Bring it on. I'd show it a thing or three. Thinking. Thinking, I thought. Stop the thinking, Altschuler.

Now Mark, the manager and head Dharma teacher, entered, and everyone gathered to hear the rules and schedule of the weekend retreat. Up at 4:30 A.M.; two sittings, with walking meditation in between; breakfast at seven; a series of meditations and chanting; household-work periods; meals in Korean Zen fashion; and a couple of short breaks—all designed to make you leap like a tiger into bed at 9:30 P.M. and sleep like a pussycat. All this was to be conducted in total silence (except the chanting, of course) with interpersonal communications, if absolutely necessary, carried on by handwritten note. Fine. I expressed myself better on paper.

The next day everything started fine. I got up at 4:15 A.M. to beat the rush to the bathroom, made it on time to the meditation hall, with its altar of incense and candles and a large statue of the Buddha, but at the end of the first forty-minute sitting my circuits began to short.

At around thirty minutes into the sitting I knew trouble was brewing. I felt like a Zen paraplegic: I couldn't sense my legs or feet. As much as they've been with me for the past thirty-three years, they were now floating somewhere, projecting astrally, perhaps, to some other plane of existence. Or maybe I had reached nirvana, that state of bodiless body, mindless mind, eternal bliss. But in nirvana I doubt if anyone bothered worrying about the way

*STEPHEN ALTSCHULER*

to get up when walking meditation began, or worse, the way to continue living alone in the woods after one's legs were amputated.

I tried to rise even though I knew from the bottom of my arches that I shouldn't; and as my pogo-stick legs and platform-shoe feet tried to support my body, over I keeled, almost landing on top of Ferris, who sat beside me. Like a newborn colt I made another attempt but knew it was too late. People began walking, and I stayed on my rump until my legs thawed. Ferris, bless her heart, stayed behind, too, out of compassion I thought then, but later I learned she had had her own troubles getting up—and she'd been a part of this coterie for about four years. Finally, I joined the slow, deliberate line of walking meditators and tried to regain my equilibrium.

But no sooner had the pins and needles left my feet than I returned to the cushion for another round with Zen—not that Zen was fighting: only my own mind contended. Years of contention, of creating dualities—right-wrong, good-bad, should-shouldn't. Zen would end the fighting. Just sit and breathe and reflect all stimuli like the clear, still, mirror-like surface of a pond. Zen would heal and reveal, would guide and illuminate. Zen would calm my anxious bird-like heart and D-tune my mind so that the bass strings would keep a steady, homogenous beat.

Yet, as I arranged my body for the next sitting, all those lofty Zen states of mind left me, and all that flooded my awareness was one thing—pain, in my crossed legs—pain that began building to a crescendo.

I never liked pain. A closet hedonist, I tried to avoid it and sought pleasure whenever possible. Yet I've often failed, and this was one of those times I wondered why I wasn't spending the weekend back at my cabin, relaxing and basking in the sun.

And fears started mounting, fears from being absolutely neurotic about physical pains and the possibility of passing out as I imagined death closing in (which formed the foundation of my phobia). Heart palpitating faster, temples pulsing with adrenalin-charged blood, extremities growing cold and damp, and the clincher: nausea. Keep it together, man, I thought. Let it pass. Zen says let it pass. Just watch it. Not to worry. No tears, no tangles. Yes, said Gautama Buddha, we suffer because we desire. So if we do not desire, we no longer suffer. Fine. I don't want nuthin' no more. No feelings. No desire. Now leave, pain and suffering.

Fortunately, the end of the sitting neared; and just as I could take no more of it and started to slump, the head Dharma teacher signaled the end of the period with a clap of the wooden *moktuk*. Time, as always, was the ultimate savior and healer.

With the end of the tension of battle, a flood of tears followed as a session of chanting began. What did all this mean? I was hurting. Plenty of suffering. Plenty of feeling. I wanted to be healed. Yes, Buddha, I desired to be healed. Yet no one was there to lay on hands but myself. I sat coiled alone, stripped of a mask that had kept my pain hidden.

As Zen masters have taught for ages, pain, like everything else, does pass. My body returned to an equilibrium, and present moments continued to be followed by more present moments, with much less pain after I discovered I could use a simple meditation bench that took pressure off my legs.

Next came the meal. Finally, I could relax, I thought. Well, not quite. Let's just say Korean Zen meals were the polar opposite of the Jewish social-event eating I'd been brought up with. I won't describe them in detail, but the meals taught a lesson in homeostasis. Everything you spooned into your one bowl must be consumed, and the whole meal lasted between five and ten minutes. That meant gulping and shoveling and, ultimately, bellyaching if you took too much.

I recorded in my journal (yes, I could not resist defying the no-writing rule) after the lunch meal of that day: "Second meal. Two pots came around. Looked the same. Bob served seconds. I looked, hesitated. He hesitated. Started back. I motioned no. He left. Beans for the soup, I think. Would've liked some. Tense at

*STEPHEN ALTSCHULER*

meals. Not used to formality. Tunnel vision when I went back to serving mat for seconds. Took a very small sweet potato. Caught sight of larger one but let it go." After the third meal I finally learned how to eat Zen-style.

Now the routine started rolling along, with the main event ahead. Late Saturday morning, while each of us was engaged in leaping while sitting, we would leave, one by one, for a personal, private interview with the head tiger, Soen-sa-nim himself. After I'd been following my breath for what seemed like forever, my turn came.

I ascended the stairs slowly, trying to remember the bowing ritual we had to perform upon entering the room. I entered, performed the bows, and sat on a cushion opposite this man whose shape and color and physiognomy reminded me of a mushroom in a deep, mossy wood. He came from a different culture, an Eastern man trying quite sincerely to convey the heart of a whole Eastern way of living to a Westerner—in this case, from South Philadelphia.

"How are you today?" he began. Two of his Western disciples, who were in training to teach, sat on either side of him.

"Fine."

"Do you have any questions?"

"Yes," and I proceeded to tell him about the previous day's battle with fear and to ask how I could overcome it, when I realized in the middle of the asking how absurd all this must have sounded to this man. I knew enough about Zen mind-murder to predict that his response would not exactly be patterned after Carl Rogers's.

"Just put it down and go straight ahead. Feelings, thoughts, fears, ideas, opinions—put them down. Only like this. Only straight ahead."

He then produced a book, a sort of Zen lesson book, handwritten in English in a script that looked like a page from a medieval Bible. It was filled with koans, or Zen riddles, that would have given even Bilbo Baggins a hard time; for example, "The mouse eats cat food, but the cat bowl is broken. What does this mean?" and "The ten thousand Dharmas return to the One. Where does the One return to?" and "Long ago Zen Master Unmun, when asked 'What is Buddha?' answered the question by saying, 'Three pounds of flax.' What does that mean?"

I, of course, heavy with mind, tried to actually answer the questions as if my eleventh-grade geometry teacher were before me: "I think the One returns to the ten thousand Dharmas," and "The mouse apparently broke the cat bowl while eating, which is symbolic of the Heart Sutra, teaching that form is emptiness, emptiness form."

These drew frowns and threatening motions from the Zen Master. But as we continued I began to learn what made the master smile: simply saying, "I don't know" or just slamming the floor with my hand or lifting one finger in the air. To this Soen-sa-nim responded approvingly and summed up the interview by saying, "Only keep this don't-know mind."

Don't know. Don't know. Don't know. I bowed and left the room. Don't know. Who am I? Don't know. Why am I studying Zen? Don't know. Why am I living in a primitive cabin in the woods? Don't know. Who's on first? Don't know. No, he's on second. Who's on first? Yes, and don't know.

Soen-sa-nim gave me no further instructions. He didn't tell me to read *The Prophet*, as a razor-slick psychic in a Holiday Inn motel room had a few years earlier. He didn't tell me to explore myself through past life readings and regressions, as an astrologer prescribed after explaining all my astrological houses from a brightly colored chart. Nor did he imply I needed to uncover layer upon layer of the accumulated garbage in my unconscious, as did a psychotherapist I saw for a number of years.

He just said put it all down and go straight ahead. No bullshit. No embellishments. No Valium. No desensitization by reciprocal inhibition. No handlebars. No Est. No rebirthing. No primal screaming. No bio-energetics. No Rolfing. No touchy-feely games. No empty-chair dialogue. No courses. No megavitamins. No Can-

*STEPHEN ALTSCHULER*

cer rising. No *I Ching*. No master swami guru messiah. Just put it all down and go straight ahead.

Put what down? Go ahead where? If I put it all down, what did I have left? Who was I?

Look here, I thought, I am Stephen Altschuler: man, writer, golf instructor, apple tree pruner, carpenter, skier, homesteader, woodsman, counselor, friend, divorcee, son, brother. Yes, but when all the names and titles settled to the bottom, who was I?

Sunday came. The home stretch. I wondered before the early morning sitting if I'd get the "Comeback of the Sesshin" award. Evening approached. A vegetarian feast was to follow some words by Soen-sa-nim. Was there a meditator among us whose mind was not invaded by the thought of that meal and the time we could take to eat it? Finally, the last gong, the last chant, the last silent walk.

I don't remember what else Soen-sa-nim said besides his first two words—"Hard training"—which he said smiling. But if he had at that point suggested a crusade to retake the Holy Land, I would've gone. He did not, however, take up his cudgel and lead us across the Red Sea, nor did he ascend the mount. Looking calm, rested, almost angelic, he just firmly and humorously reaffirmed his teaching.

People asked fewer questions at this closing talk. Perhaps they were just tired. Or maybe a collective realization arose that silent mind transcends thinking mind. Personally, I was exhausted and really wanted to get to the meal, at which I stuffed myself thoroughly and gabbed the smallest talk I could muster.

"Hi," said Soen-sa-nim as he sat down next to me.

"Hi."

"Good cake?"

"Very delicious."

And then the leaving, as Ferris and I prepared to drive back to New Hampshire and a welcomed return to my usual daily schedule in the woods. On the porch I turned to say goodbye to Bob, one of the residents of the center. "I'm glad you stopped by," he waved, as we turned and smiled at his perfect understatement of the Zen approach to life.

# DIGGING

As Zen training demonstrated with sitting still and watching the breath, sometimes the simplest of tasks took on universal proportions, especially when the task at hand resisted as if it had an intelligence of its own and was trying to teach a lesson of sorts. Now, back at the cabin, I discovered this first-hand with digging a root cellar, a project I would recommend if you had some deep, dark karma to work out. With the ground thawed and softened by spring rains and with winter looming like the Loch Ness monster (I hadn't seen it yet but just knew it was there, a mere six months away), I concluded that a root cellar would insure my very survival.

Could it be that nature just needed a good laugh that day and hadn't intended a lesson at all? If so, this prime sucker leapt right in with the tenacity and I.Q. of a bulldog. Some great ideas should remain great ideas, this one included, but, as with many aspects of living in the woods, it took doing it for me to get smart about it.

As for my inner life, living in the woods alone and isolated wrested some old wounds to the surface—leftover wounds from the severe phobic reaction, wounds that made me feel as if I would fall apart or get terribly anxious if I talked to or looked anyone in the eye too long. I don't know: maybe the Zen retreat opened the floodgates too much, too soon. Tears would well up suddenly and flow like a stream from unknown pools. My neighbor old Tom told me once that there was a stream nearby that flowed only in the morning and around noon— other times, nothing. He simply ascribed this to Nature; it must be Nature. Like the pools that fed that stream, my tears seemed to be always there. And like the stream itself, they sometimes flowed and sometimes didn't. Tom might have explained this the same way.

I kept active, though, with a schedule that included physical work, writing, walking, and meditation. A forced activity, really, in order to avoid a depression that I knew was harder to cope with than acute anxiety. I took care of business, which in the woods often meant hauling and fixing . . . and digging.

Digging consumed a lot of my time and energy—digging through obstinate, unyielding, and downright contrary New Hampshire soil and stone. I was digging a root cellar, but what I was digging at times felt incidental to the digging itself. Digging is one of the oldest construction activities around, and I now knew why. It put you so close to earth, to roots, to soil. It brought to mind my childhood and times of intense concentration on sandbox projects. No end product there, just digging, and in the digging, being. But as an adult I had to have a purpose for digging, or some work-ethic folks might have called me shiftless or unproductive . . . or the ultimate, counterproductive—a word some politician made up for anything that opposed his own ideas.

So if anyone asked me *what* I was digging, I said truthfully, but in as understated a manner as possible and with no further detail, a root cellar—a pronouncement that got them off my back and discouraged any conversation—common in the country—on the wheres, whys, and hows (or is it howls?) of holes.

Most people would not understand, but for me, more important and critical than the end product or the work ethic was stones, those sentinels of the soil that made digging digging, and, in the following episode, made digging seem, on cosmic levels, even more than digging.

A builder friend of mine liked and studied stones a great deal. He said the great thing about them was that they had a different perspective every way you turned them. He was talking about construction stones, out-of-the-ground stones, conquered stones that lay in a heap, part of the victorious digger's spoils. The stones I dealt with had only one perspective as they leered up like lions, holding—*literally* holding—their ground.

These stones sat as dedicated and tenacious as the sit-in demonstrators in the South in the early sixties, or the nuclear-plant protesters in the North in the late seventies. The cause stones fought for, though, had nothing to do with civil rights or risky energy sources: it had to do with holes, holes that stones did not want dug.

One stone I encountered deserves special mention because what ensued for about six hours will hereafter be known as the Battle of Backwoods Cabin . . . at least, in the book of my own history. It started with a guerrilla scouting mission with my pick, penetrating the earth and discovering that the enemy was much larger than anticipated. A number of forays around the perimeter showed this stone to be of boulder proportions. Open warfare commenced as I entered the fray with what I hoped would be even bolder proportions. I jabbed and picked and shoveled and crowbarred, and at one point retreated . . . for lunch. Then back to the battlefield. I thrust forward, then fell back, considering a call for reinforcements—

strongarms on the other side of the mountain. But no, the struggle, for me, had to be as always: alone. Me and my own mind and body against something I'd defined as an opposing force other than me fighting against me, but that was, in reality, nothing but me.

Anyway, existentialism notwithstanding, I finally pried the behemoth loose. I relaxed. I'd won, hadn't I? Just a mopping-up operation remained, right? Well, for the next four hours, I tried every device and idea imaginable to get that rock out of there: levers, ropes, chains, pushing, pulling. At one point I even tried levitating it out—an act of psychic desperation. Then, in a flash of Napoleonic insight, I thought of my car jack. Rigging up a kind of scaffolding over the hole, I wrapped a chain around the vanquished rock and proceeded to jack up the mini-mountain. My Rube Goldberg device came close to success on the first try, but as I tried to swing the rock out, wham! Kerplotz! Thump! Total collapse. Everything—jack, scaffolding, rock, me—lay at the bottom of the bloody hole.

But patience, persistence, and a basically optimistic view of life, titrated from my father, prevailed, so I kept at it. Over and over, like Sisyphus, I grappled with that implacable hunk of granite for the next couple of hours. Until at long last everything fitted together: the jack, time, speed, mass multiplied by a constant squared, wind velocity, my spirit guides, the planets, my right hand properly aligned with my left—whatever determined the workings of this mysterious universe.

There it sat, and there sat I, face to face, in peace, like two old friends after a good, out-in-the-open fight. It had become that—an old friend, a piece of myself, really—struggling, striving, lifting, collapsing, struggling, and rising again. The boundary between me and that rock blurred as the attention I brought to the task made me forget why I was trying to move that mass, and, in the process, broke through the wall of ego—the wall of wanting things to be a certain way, the wall of thinking of where I was going instead of doing what I was doing, a wall that normally separated me from life, from living.

*STEPHEN ALTSCHULER*

For with attention and concentration on the matter at hand, life appeared, advancing over the fortifications of the intractable self. Life endured, but sometimes the activity of thinking—particularly, dysfunctional thinking with fear, worry, and anticipation—obscured the view of life and the feeling of aliveness I had, just standing there.

The act of attention called digging could breach those defenses and reinforce remembering the marrow. Experienced in its essence, stripped of its purpose, digging became as pure and unencumbered as each of us the day we were born into this vast, awesome, and beautiful world. Pure, because it had the potential for attending only to the moment—attending to digging . . . and living.

# 4 SUMMER

As summer drew near and my mind settled into my surroundings, the longer days gave me time to enjoy where I was living. I could easily get too caught up in work or tasks or plans and forget to look around to see my surroundings. Since conditioning and socialization had led me so far from nature—including my inner nature—I needed to make a conscious effort to notice it, to feel it, to remember it. In cities, where I grew up and spent most of my time, I only read about nature or drove to it and then drove out of it, back to something I always seemed to be late for.

But at the cabin, time, or my perception of it, moved slower, thus allowing my senses to operate as they were intended to operate. And at this time of year all the added daylight revealed everything around me, so my mind could not deny what my senses experienced. No matter how busy I wanted to be, eventually it all got done with the longer day, and *finally I could do nothing but sit back and take it all in, taking time to think and reflect on things.*

*June 1: "I sighted a beaver again tonight. The first time was yesterday with Al over at Beaver Pond. Apparently, beavers had just moved in and had already dammed up the outlets, raising the pond's level.*

*"There's something about beavers that moves me: the way they go about their business quietly and steadily, the way they get the job done through ingenuity and patience and perseverance. Some people have those qualities, but all beavers have them. To me, their natural selection, their evolution, is quite advanced—they know exactly what their task is and are equipped to accomplish it, and all do accomplish it (if they're not killed or driven out by people along the way)."*

*I watched that beaver much of the summer, noting that it had probably advanced more along on the evolutionary scale than I, for it knew exactly what it was placed on earth to achieve, and without the slightest hesitation it did what it learned early on to do. I, on the other hand, wasn't so sure of my place in life and lolled about that summer doing some deep thinking . . . and deep seeing.*

T he long winter and cold spring accentuated the summer for me. Finally, the delicate, almost frail hands of summer grasped the hemisphere and blew warm breezes for a couple of short months. I took time to sit back, feel the sun, wear T-shirts and wide-brim hats, and listen to the music of the forest. With the solstice came a full symphony of sound: birds and crickets and frogs and bees and other buzzing creatures bellowed and chirped and hummed and squeaked as the warm wind played harmony for the whole band. The spring saw birth—an awakening, a stretching, an excited tremolo. The summer was vibrant and verdant maturity, expansive,

*STEPHEN ALTSCHULER*

blossoming, showing off its finery as it strutted and danced like an uninhibited mummer.

For me the summer brought an easiness that the other seasons lacked. No wood to cut or burn. Less cooking and dishwashing. More fresh and raw fruits and vegetables. More walking and seeing and hearing and smelling—ah the smelling!—of warm, fresh breezes, of roses in town gardens, of electrified air after a thunderstorm, of a skunk flexing its scent glands, of the dank moss hugging the banks of the creek where I dipped my cup and sometimes my feet.

This first summer here filled me with excitement and anticipation. It filled me with wonder shaped and heightened by birds—summer birds, soaring hawks, phoebes fluttering in front of my loft window, chickadees and jays vying for feeding territory. After the winter they began to trickle back in spring like wanderers, travelers returning home. They came home rejuvenated, full of chitter and chatter, full of life and flight. Flight—that more than anything made birds the envy of man. We'll never have self-propelled flight, so it will always remain a dream, a vision, a metaphor.

I sat outside my cabin and watched the summer birds fly. The warm winds let me dream, and my thoughts and spirit ascended, unencumbered, touching down, then taking off again. No wonder their songs and warbles were so clear and alive. I lay back and dreamed—lazy daydreams, and more expansive dreams that were spawned within all the time that summer allowed.

The winter would mean survival and keeping warm and attending to everyday tasks. But the summer had let me gather together my inner resources and project and reflect into life and time ahead. Was I content with the way my life was going? Where did I want to be in ten years? What if I had only six months to live? Would I be doing what I was now doing?—questions that seemed irrelevant to other seasons, since then I was doing exactly what I needed to be doing to deal with their more immediate demands.

Summer, though, indulged the senses. Its warmth and sun and

humidity directed thoughts to the future. Maybe that accounted for less getting accomplished, less task orientation. The body could relax more, yet, for the mind, it could also be a more anxiety-producing time: fewer maintenance functions, yet more thought, which I knew could get me into trouble if most of that thought dwelled on anticipating, planning, and projecting. And I knew, too, that anytime I left the moment, I became unsettled. Was I content? Where was I headed? Did this woods life have meaning and purpose? Summer was almost defined by self-indulgence, so these were questions I would ask and re-ask during the hot, lethargic days ahead. No pressure to come up with answers now. No need, quite yet, to figure things out. Birds up there needed seeing. Trees out there needed hugging. Flowers all around needed smelling. Waddling skunks somewhere needed smiling at. Beavers over at the pond needed marveling at. And summer itself needed my lazy mind, swimming with questions. But not answers, not just then.

# FOOD

I had, like most urbanites, taken food, and where it came from, for granted. Satisfying my stomach's heart desire merely meant popping over to the market or convenience store. That tack veered about 180 degrees from the source of food a few short generations ago, when people knew and grew their food supply well, even to the timing of when to plant the seeds.

I had dabbled with gardening, but with a refrigerator and freezer had never considered choosing foods according to the seasons vis-a-vis my body's needs. The thought never dawned on me that in winter the extra fat needed for the cold would be preserved by that same cold, and that the salads I craved in summer required a cool spot but no refrigeration in the long, hot days, provided I used what I bought in a reasonable amount of time. As a city dweller I was out of touch with the cycles of the seasons and ate particular foods not because I needed them but because electricity allowed me to preserve them.

*In the woods, without the so-called conveniences, I began to re-connect with ancient rhythms of pre-refrigerated humankind. This new view of food brought spirit, adventure, and joy back to eating, food gathering, and storage, as well as a practical awareness of what I needed for nourishment in any given season. I was looking at myself and my life differently—experimenting and trying new ways of being and feeling, and paying close attention to the supposedly mundane, but actually rich, details of daily life.*

## THE GARDEN

A snowstorm in May, spring temperatures that went up and down like a high-rise elevator, and a drought in June hadn't made it the greatest year for gardens. Some insects, like cutworms, seemed to call in every troop from every reserve unit in the country, and potato beetles came along as reinforcements.

As for my garden, I could boast the most organic plot in the area—that is, every living organic critter that ever chewed on a lettuce leaf stalked that small plot, armed, or maybe mouthed, with appetites that would have made Wimpy's seem like Audrey Hepburn's. These critters included moles, rabbits, mice, porcupines, and the blinking glutton of my all-night-diner garden, the woodchuck—or, as he was also known for his looks as well as his culinary habits, the groundhog.

In fact, a family of woodchuck neighbors came out every night and set up their best china and silver, tucked in their bibs, selected the evening's menu, then devoured anything and everything green and crisp with the exception of grass and weeds.

Now every time I met someone knowledgeable on this subject, I asked them what to do about woodchucks. A sampling of some of the answers included: throw bombs in their holes, after they go

*STEPHEN ALTSCHULER*

in; trap them, either alive or dead; build a good stout fence about ten feet below the ground and twenty feet above—sometimes electrified; or scare them away by burying glass bottles up to the top, creating a low, whistling sound when the wind blows (I guess if the wind wasn't blowing they might stub their toes on the bottles in the dark). Oh, and one guy suggested just out-and-out shooting them.

Well, my response was a hundred percent: I didn't heed any of them. Seemed all of these people making suggestions missed an important point: woodchucks had as much right to poke around in that garden as I did. That woodchuck neighbor of mine was there long before I arrived. Anyway, my gripe didn't concern territory. It was a lot more basic than that, summed up in a poem/song I wrote for that woodchuck neighbor of mine.

### Woodchuck Eats My Garden

Woodchuck eats my garden,
eats it night and day.
Chewin' on a lettuce plant,
Sittin' on some hay.
Now, I don't mind you chewin',
I can spare a plant or two.
But if you're gonna help yourself,
I wish you'd help me, too.

I tell him, "Woodchuck, grab a shovel.
Woodchuck lift a hoe.
I've planted all your favorites.
Ain't askin' for no dough.
But if you're gonna nibble,
Then lend a helpin' hand.
Then you and I can live in peace,
and share this piece of land."

Unfortunately, the shovel and hoe continued sitting in their places, touched only by me. I still had hope, though, that I would get some cooperation from this critter—a kind of faith in a universal sense of fair play, faith in the law of give-and-take. Of course, sometimes those laws broke down, even with humans.

A few years ago a human stole most of the tomatoes in another of my gardens in another place, and the only things he left behind were footprints. But generally, living things, other than politicians, did cooperate with one another. So I just kept sitting outside my cabin strumming and singing that song to a recalcitrant woodchuck, hoping one day the critter would come walking up, pulling on little paw-sized work gloves, and asking, "Where's the shovel, Jack?"

## EATING

Since that local woodchuck gourmet just about leveled my garden, I'd have to wait until next year to reach any kind of self-sufficiency with my food supply. Besides, since I moved to the cabin in mid-May, with all the fixing up that needed doing I didn't get the garden in until the end of the month. So I didn't have a lot invested in it.

I thought a great deal about food before moving to the woods. I wanted to let the seasons and the lack of refrigeration, running water, and electricity shape my diet, not have my diet force me into conveniences I really didn't want. I liked that back-to-the-land Bible, Helen and Scott Nearing's *Living the Good Life*; I liked their style of a minimum of cooking and of eating mostly fresh vegetables, fruits, nuts, and grains. Unlike meat, which usually churned up my stomach and ultimately over-strained the planet as well, these foods agreed with my system.

So, for one thing, I kept a gallon jar of raw and toasted nuts on the table right next to my swivel chair. And every time I got a hunger pang, which was pretty often, I wheeled around and dipped into that heavenly mixture. I hadn't come across any snack quite like it: I never tired of tasting it, it didn't bloat me, and it gave my system all sorts of nutrients. I'd like to have grown those nuts, but I didn't even have lettuce in my garden, let alone nut trees.

No, like most people I bought most of my food, but with one difference: Whenever possible, I didn't shop at supermarkets. Supermarkets made me dizzy. I think the combination of the bright lights and the avalanche of bold-colored boxes, the floors with arrows saying "One Way," the whir and buzz of cash registers, and the rush-hour congestion of shopping carts overwhelmed my senses. That was it, I think—the whole thing reminded me of driving on a busy highway at five o'clock on a Friday evening in the middle of a hot July. My stomach got all tied up in knots, my head got spacey, and my vision started to blur. And then someone behind the counter was expecting me to know how much potato salad I wanted. I just couldn't handle supermarkets. So I got my food from the little store in town or from the fruit and vegetable stand or the food co-op or from friends' gardens. I preferred the values inherent in those food outlets.

But thinking ahead to winter, I took some steps to become more self-sufficient, like digging a root cellar. It would be my subterranean refrigerator, only I wouldn't have to worry about defrosting it or paying the repairman fifteen dollars just to come in and look at it (and I mean just look at it and declare it a refrigerator and tell me it wasn't plugged in). I hoped to store a winter's supply of fruits and vegetables. So this got me closer to my food supply, more intimate with what would eventually be a part of me, and I liked the values inherent in that as well.

I still cooked—on an old kerosene stove and oven I bought for five bucks from a guy in the nearby town of Westmoreland. Mostly, I made my favorite meal—sauteed vegetables and brown rice. But I did much less cooking than when I lived in conventional environs. I reasoned that less cooking meant less cleaning, and less cleaning meant more time for enjoyable pursuits like writing and reading and hiking. Washing dishes had never been my forte, and stuffing them into a dishwasher never washed with me either. So I resolved to cook less and eat most of my meals from one wooden bowl or the pot I cooked with.

Just try this on a warm, early summer day, as I often did: slice up a ripe peach, a banana, an orange, or just about any fruit you have on hand, throw in some blueberries and chunks of watermelon, sprinkle in a handful of toasted, unsalted nuts, add some raisins and a dash of cinnamon. And then dribble on liberally the supreme nectar of the northern woods: dark maple syrup, the cheapest you can find, like Grade C. That kind has a stronger maple flavor than the expensive stuff. Get yourself a wooden bowl and make it your special fruit bowl. Don't wash it too thoroughly. Let that pure maple syrup soak in and darken the natural grain of the wood.

Food, a meal, became a sensual event at the cabin. It was an offering to my body and a reminder that I was one of the more fortunate beings on this earth who could choose and select and cull out any food I wished, who could swing around in his swivel chair and dip his hand into heaven.

# 6
# OF MICE AND ME

Not only did I have to take a closer look at my eating habits in the first few months, but my sleeping patterns, previously protected by the Maginot lines of urban life—such as lock-tight houses or apartments, built on solid foundations, in clean, well-sewered neighborhoods—were now interrupted by mice scampering and scratching in the walls just a tail's length from my head in the cabin's sleeping loft. They seemed to know just when I was beginning to doze off, for at that point I'm sure I could hear them snickering and giggling as they raced through the fiberglass insulation.

So with summer heat and humidity bearing down upon me, coupled with mice-induced sleep deprivation, I began to scrutinize grumpily what I was doing with my life. I considered myself an educated, creative man, capable of great things (I always imagined), now holed up in a shack (in other moods, I called it "cabin" and before that "cottage") in the north woods, contemplating killing mice. Was this the sum total *of the civilized learning and experience I had accumulated up to this point?*

*Well . . . yes! And I couldn't have had a better classroom for test-ing my values and morals. Mice in my walls forced me out of my intellect and into the core of my being where the spirit of a human being forms and develops. Mice in my walls granted no time for theorizing or contemplating, as in former college days, or even calling for the extermi-nator, as in former urban days. Noisy mice didn't fit into theories, and exterminators normally didn't make house calls a mile into the woods. So without formulas or precedents or an instruction manual I had to figure out on my own another odd configuration of living in the coun-try. Such grappling is health food for the soul.*

I had a hard time deciding what to do about the mice in my cabin when I moved in. They must have deemed it as totally their territory, seeing me as just passing through, because they were running up and down and around this place, checking out my food-stuffs as if they were commodity buyers at the Chicago Board of Trade. They tunneled and burrowed in the wall and ceiling insu-lation, and judging by their speed they must have had a system of conduits that would make the subway in Boston look like a game of croquet.

Now, I didn't mind field mice as long as they stayed in fields. They looked sort of cute and seemed a lot cleaner than city mice, who could spread disease, since they lounged about in garbage, and in the winter they even claimed squatter's rights in stoves. In fact, one time, when I was making London broil in a college apartment in Philadelphia, I opened the broiler and out came this mouse, almost running over my hand. So in the past I knew exactly and decisively what to do with city mice: I'd kill them with any variety of weapon.

STEPHEN ALTSCHULER

But here at the cabin the only crimes I could pin on these backwoods mice were wall-scratching and trespassing, neither of these falling into the capital-offense category. Yes, the scratching kept me awake at night, and it was now my territory, but these things didn't threaten my physical well-being.

Generally, I had been of a pacifist nature, although if something or someone threatened me physically, I'd defend myself. But with these prototypes of Annette Funicello and the Mouseketeers, every time I saw one dart past or peer out through a crack in the wall I'd start thinking of head Mouseketeer Jimmy, singing M-I-C—see ya real soon—K-E-Y—why? because we like you—M-O-U-S-E. Not easy thinking of death and annihilation and blood and battle when I had those memories going through my mind.

But I hit a point when I reached an inner limit—a point of no return when I left my city-ness behind and became more of a woods-man—a point when I stopped thinking Mouseketeers and started thinking mousetraps. But it wasn't so cut-and-dried, not as simple as going to a hardware store and buying a couple of Victors, loading them with cheese, and setting the trigger. No, like that humane, alternative animal trap, I Had-A-Heart to consider.

So I designed and built my own version of the Have-A-Heart trap that would catch them alive, allowing transport and complete resettlement, I hoped, a few miles away. If I had a drawing board, however, I would have gone back to it, because the damn thing didn't work. A good thing, too, because since then I took the murderous route and killed about ten or eleven of them and would've been spending most of my time on the road.

So I went to the hardware store and bought a smaller version of the kind of trap that helped America extinguish some species completely and make outlaws of others, as it built its farms, ranches, roads, cities, and suburbs.

Choosing to mete out sudden death with a whack-trap put me through some changes at first. After that first kill I had to do some serious rationalizing, which went as follows: I lived in the woods.

The woods could be dangerous and risky. Death takes place as much as life. Those mice were in my home. And they would defend their home as I would defend mine. How did that sound? Pretty neat and logical, huh?

Well, the next few days were as anxiety-ridden as I had felt since working in a state prison a few years earlier. Deep feelings of remorse and guilt stirred and were trying to get out but couldn't find an opening. Death really floored me. Whether involving a close relative or friend—or, yes, even a field mouse—just when I thought I was getting it all together death would tap me on the shoulder and say, "Ha, Ha, you thought you could be a tough guy and ignore me again, huh? Well, no way, Buster, ignore me and you'll have to ignore life."

Ignore death and I would have to ignore life. For me, here in the woods, both grew as branches from the same ancient tree. Every moment of every day, something was born, something grew, and something died, and what died spawned the next seed of the next birth. No separation existed here, just the woods, and the woods *were* life and death. A tree didn't think, "Uh, oh! Here comes a lightning storm," or the beaver didn't dread the bulldozer coming to fill in his pond, or the mouse didn't sit around fretting, "Oh, my God! Those traps make me so nervous, I need a tranquilizer."

There might be an instinctive fear, but it happened at the moment of danger, not three weeks before or after. The woodchuck whose home was next to my cabin didn't worry about taking a midnight stroll or leaving his hole open. Living things in the woods lived whole lifetimes in a moment. A moment was born, lived, and then passed away and died, leaving behind the seed of a new moment. Living things, aside from humans, distinguished no past or future, no anticipatory fear of dying. Life in the woods confronted, dealt with, and worked through death and rebirth every moment.

And now, I, too, lived in the woods. And as I became more a part of these environs, as I struggled to leave more of my cityness behind, I, too, began to know the unity of life and death. I, too, began to live lifetimes within the inhaling and exhaling of each breath.

Of course, all this offered no consolation to the mice in my walls, who kept wondering what the problem was that prompted capital punishment. They were being themselves—just mice running through the insulation—which was supposed to be what the universe liked: beings being themselves. "It's not right," they might have reasoned if they could reason. "Why are we getting clobbered?"

I would have had no good answer to give my mice housemates, if they could have understood it. I would have squirmed and fidgeted in my chair, looked at their cute little ears between the cracks in the wall, and retreated into some form of escape or denial as I continued to bait the traps and rid the cabin, and my life, of their presence.

And bait I did, until the scratching in the walls stopped, their little ears were no longer seen, and my foodstuffs once again remained intact. A strange nostalgia came over me, though. In some inexplicable way, like having post-divorce doubts, I missed the little critters. Maybe their predictability was reassuring. Maybe their noises made me less lonely. Maybe I just felt closer to the woods and all the wildness in it. Or maybe I simply could not separate them from Annette and Jimmy as I lifted the trap's baler and dropped them into the compost heap.

But nostalgia notwithstanding, I did not invite them back. I apologized to their species and acknowledged my evolutionary position as a clumsy oaf of an Earth inhabitant, incapable of living in total harmony with my fellow Earthlings. I even grieved for them, but after a few good nights' sleep, I was glad they were gone.

# LIVING ALONE

As time went on and late summer days shortened, the weight of living totally alone in an isolated woodland grew heavier. On rare occasions a friend would drop by unannounced, and sometimes, once a week or so, I would drive to town or drop in on friends. Every couple of days I'd walk to the mailbox on the main county road and chat with neighbors if they happened to be puttering around their yards. As for the cats (and I'll tell you about them soon), they served as sort of comic companions—court jesters—but their antics, or even their climbing my lap, though nurturing, didn't fully replace human contact and conversation.

To add to the aloneness, August saw the nights grow colder, giving a prick of what lay ahead, and my swirling thoughts took me to the "dark and lonely night" beginnings of bad novels. In the city distractions flashed wherever I turned: I could flick on the TV, call a friend, go to a café, see a movie, or just walk down a busy shopping avenue. Even the traffic noise was somehow reassuring—that others of my species were close by, and although most of them didn't care a whit for my welfare, I had the illusion I wasn't alone and so was protected from what I learned early on was not normal.

Here, though, the instant antidotes to being alone were less available. This lack meant, that first summer, more anxiety as feelings of isolation, abandonment, and a doubting of trust in myself rose to the surface. But as time went on and I faced myself more, in all my masks, those feelings were exposed to be not feelings at all but sleights of hand my ego feigned to keep me from knowing and liking myself—illusions that kept me from participating fully in life.

Late that first summer I wrote in my journal, which I'd been keeping for ten years: "A blank page stares back at me intently. The shadow of my hand, cast by kerosene light, covers the pen strokes, forcing me, almost, to use my heart rather than eyes and head. In my autumn years, living here plucks the strings of my aloneness—the bass-string background to what I can only hope will be the harmony and the dance."

When people heard I lived alone in the woods they invariably asked, "Don't you get lonely?" as if living alone were synonymous with loneliness. Loneliness was not the consequence but the malady of living alone. For living alone was itself a positive action on this inner journey.

The malady had struck me at times—on Saturday nights alone in the cabin, on long rainy days when the only thing to do was hole up with a cat on my knee—times when I would miss

*STEPHEN ALTSCHULER*

that almost instant contact that town living and a telephone afforded. I would then turn for solace and industry to my writing or a good book. Yet those lonely feelings, like post-nasal drip, often continued.

At times like those I was tempted to chase away lonely-itis with such external drugs as getting into my car and driving somewhere, or walking to see friends, or doing some make-work project, or picking up my guitar and singing for awhile. But when I stayed with my loneliness, gave it free rein and watched it swirl around my head, I could understand and accept it. I could let it in without hindrance, and then let it go.

One of the opportunities available with this woods life was the chance to rediscover ignored and sometimes shadowy aspects of myself and the feelings that got stirred when "lonely" related to some of those aspects. Those feelings made up as much a part of me as the joy I felt when hiking over the mountain, or the anger when one of my cats devoured some freshly-made cookies I forgot to put away. And when I let in the sadness and loss connected with loneliness, I saw it was not as scary as I anticipated. For loneliness evinced past memories painfully lamented, or the vision of some future dream too far beyond my grasp to be realized in the present. Loneliness, like those things, was not solid.

I didn't get lonely very often in my cabin. My situation differed from the one I experienced when the din of city life seemed to heighten the expectations and frustrations of my social life. Out there, I lived closer to my core, more balanced and centered. I chose to be alone and accepted the responsibility it entailed, a responsibility and commitment that involved trusting in the relatedness of each element of a perfect web.

One cool evening, after I had been sitting meditation, a fly perched on my knee, preening its wings, totally comfortable with itself and apparently with me. Had it no fear I would swat it? Had it no anxiety about impending death? What awesome, inherent trust this living thing had for me and the universe it lived in. The fly traveled alone, with great courage. A Buddha's courage. This fly that was as alive as I seemed to be connected to me for those moments in a bond that transcended species and ego and thinking mind. Could I trust as that fly trusted? Could I feel such a connection with all that existed?

Living alone meant not being lonely. Approached sincerely and with vigor, it could be a vehicle of growth that would inoculate me against the ravages of loneliness. Yet living alone for a time, being with myself in a deep sense, felt risky. It neccessitated stepping off safe ground to a place with fewer familiar anchors to make me feel more secure. And stepping off that ground heightened the dichotomy between my small self—my thoughts, my fears, my patterns and life-scripts, my past pains—and the truth of a more magnanimous Self—a grander part of me that knew only love and connection. That larger Self, particularly present when alone, felt alien and dangerous, though, like any uncharted territory. So I resisted steering in the direction of its wisdom and power.

But in order for me to really get closer to others and the living environment, in order for relationships, marriages, friendships to be healthy and satisfying, that element of aloneness was important for blazing a path that led to comfort with both the smaller self and the bigger picture of a larger Self—a True Self, as some teachers called it.

In mid-month, as I sat on a sawbuck in front of the cabin feeling the warm summer breeze, watching huge cumulus clouds drift by, I remembered a time when I felt I couldn't make it on my own—a time when the way I saw myself depended on the way others saw me and the way I looked and the way my career was progressing. At that time, I was consumed with a phobia that made me want to flee, not only from others but from my own mind.

A residue of that time remained, but gradually, living alone in the woods became an affirmation that I was not what others thought

I was, or was not even what I thought I once was. Perhaps because it stripped life down to its bare essentials and showed me, despite my internal rantings of predicted doom, the ease and freedom such nakedness could bring, living alone affirmed that I needn't go beyond my own skin to discover, and be in kinship with, the universe.

# JUST BEFORE THE
# FALL EQUINOX

With summer's end, reflections on loneliness and living alone became passé for me as the immediacy of winter loomed. Anyway, by then I'd gotten used to being alone and all the introspection it spawned.

Fall had always been my favorite time of year. The embrace of sweaters nurtured me, and the shorter days seemed natural to one with some northern European blood. In New England the display of colors dazzled the eyes, but in that year it felt as if I'd seen them for the first time. For a big difference existed between looking at the country from the outside, as the "leafers" saw it from their tour buses up from the city, and looking at the country from the inside. More senses came into play. And more of my spirit intermingled with the nature spirits that seemed to be dancing a final dance before the cold descended and made everything still and dormant.

Living alone in a deep-country cabin, witnessing such vitality and movement was a benediction. I loved the touch of chill on my bearded face, getting busy again, cutting wood, stocking up, going to sleep early, and waking up to a bolt of crystal sunlight through the red and yellow trees.

But in early September, just before the autumnal equinox, my view of that fall unalterably, and tragically, changed. The state police tracked me down through the radio station I was connected with at the time to tell me my ex-wife had committed suicide. It had been two years since we separated and a year since the divorce, but we had shared a sizable portion of early adulthood, and the news shook me deeply. She had taken an overdose of medicine for which she knew that no known antidote existed. Depression had overwhelmed her defenses, as a friend of hers later told me. I went to her funeral—the first one I'd ever attended—then hurried back to the solitude and embrace of the woods, where I sat long hours in reflective meditation. I'd been studying Zen Buddhism for about a year.

Somehow, although I didn't realize it at the time, her death resulted in an important life turning point for me. As the great psychotherapist and writer Stanley Keleman put it in his book Living Your Dying: " . . . the other side of endings is the gateway to new power and new relationships, to a new way of being in the world. Dying is a new way of being in the world. An ending establishes a relationship between ourselves and the unknown."

Four days earlier, I had written in my journal, about myself but as if I were affected by what was brewing in her, since she and I had been so connected: "I feel sad now. It's grief of the start of losing the self. So scary. The unknown. I don't know anything other than self. Yet before I give it up, I have to face it totally. What does that mean? What am I after I do that? Is it leaving the spire and floating in space?" This last question referred to a recurring dream I had at age eleven, shortly after my grandmother died, in which I felt that if I lost contact between my big toe and a spire in space I would float away and die, float away like a balloon full of feelings.

*After this devastating event I went deeper into nature—my own and the one that surrounded me.*

In mid-September I noticed the subtle signs marking the change from summer to fall—the mellowing and yellowing of that deep summer green, the nights just nip enough for another layer of blanket, and the early mornings cool enough for a bright flannel shirt. This last breath before the autumnal equinox signified a kind of bleary-eyed awakening of what was to come. Activity quickened. I dug my root cellar and winter well, knowing that in a short time the ground would be frozen. All around the community, house builders hammered a little faster, respecting the crazy-quilt nature of New England weather that could let loose with snow well before the December solstice. And small animals hastened to stock their winter supply of food.

This frenzied activity sometimes bordered on confusion and panic. Even my neighbor woodchuck seemed affected: he saw me one day out near the garden, turned to run away, and ran smack into a big rock. Poor critter was stunned for a moment before he got his bearings back.

All this activity; yet the early fall prescribed a retreat from the open, expansive summer, a time of maturing, of harvesting, then wilting, and finally being still and dormant. Maybe that was why my insides felt so unsettled. My dreams had spawned all sorts of unsavory characters trying in various ways to do me in. And in my waking hours, innocent stargazing often turned into getting scared thinking about infinity and death. Or thoughts of the approaching winter crept in, and long nights of being here alone with only myself to face.

After so many years of city and town living, I felt separate from the cycles of nature, something I talked about with a friend of mine on the other side of the mountain. We were gazing at trees and wondering aloud how marvelous it would be to be like one of these remarkable living things.

The cycle and life of a tree epitomized clarity and naturalness. Each season, what you saw mirrored exactly what was happening. Its leaves were born, grew, and flourished, then wilted and died, spiraling to the earth to add nutrients that spawned new birth. The tree itself lived on. Yes, some died, but most lived on through the ravaging winter, dormant, still, resolute, trusting instinctively that the warmer winds of spring would eventually caress it. The tree didn't fear losing its leaves, nor did it anticipate the next warm summer sun. It just lived—rooted, taking in, coping with whatever nature presented in each moment. It worried not about identity crises, nor did it concern itself with vanity or wonder about where its next meal was coming from. It simply took its place in nature and grew and breathed and swayed and creaked . . . and finally died, died like one of its offspring leaves—silently, gently, with dignity—died exactly the same way it lived.

If only I could have been as clear as a tree and as trusting that nature really *was* Mother Nature—trusting that if I just reacted to life freely and openly, nature would provide. But maybe that would come with time. Right then, the woods and its cycles were so new to me, new in the sense that they had been there inside of me, but I was only then opening myself to the experience.

It would probably take a long time for me to be like a tree— a lot more frenetic activity at the pregnant pause between summer and fall. More scared feelings and bad dreams; yet maybe the being was in the becoming.

STEPHEN ALTSCHULER

# THE APPROACHING WINTER

In the north, of all the seasons winter got the most attention, usually in the form of dread. As the colors of October faded and the month drew to an end, I looked at my woodpile, thinking naively that it would last until March. It did not last that long, but at this point in my country education, it seemed enough.

All my preparations—food, clothing, transportation, water, light—seemed enough but were not, for when I was living in the city, enough meant just enough until it was time to go the store again. There, winter had been not a survival issue but a temporary nuisance that involved more clothing. It had been cold and sometimes snowy, but life proceeded as it had through most of the year, with occasional blips during blizzards.

In this cabin, though, I was more exposed to weather, manifested by the increasingly visible sky as leaves died and fell in late fall. The magnitude of a wilderness winter was not in my experience, but within two months I would know it well.

Of my ex-wife's death, I continued to be deeply affected, acknowledging some feelings, stuffing others, and getting a cold in the process. A couple of weeks later, after speaking to her best friend, I wrote: "I understand better. She lived with a lot of pain—always. Emotional, physical. Always something. She made a choice. She said she might [commit suicide]. I thought she could. I stayed away. I felt some guilt but had to stay away in order to keep myself alive. A part of me loved her, though, and always will. She got into my gut, and although I sought to get her out it was a futile seeking.

"We talked once—half jokingly—of double suicide. It could've happened. We were both in very bad shape. If I had had something physical to deal with, as she did [a deteriorating muscular condition], I don't think I would've made it. Neither of us was prepared for the hard emotional storms of living."

I know I wasn't prepared—witness my unreadiness for the coming winter at this cabin. On the edge. Just enough . . . maybe.

Since I came to this cabin in the spring, only one thought, one anticipation, has been able to propel me from the present into the future. Call it a specter or a talisman, a rogue or a saint, a healer or a ravager, everyone I came in contact with here mentioned it to the point of obsession. Our conversation usually went like this:

"How long have you been living up here?" they asked.

"Since May," I replied.

"Oh, you mean you haven't been through a winter yet," they retorted, in tones that implied, "You poor, misguided neophyte."

Winter—at least, the thought of it—had been with me since the day I arrived. Even the hottest, muggiest July days prompted storekeepers and neighbors to comment, "In a few months we'll be wishing it was this hot again." And the preparation required: wood hauling, cutting, and splitting; root-cellar and winter-well digging; squirreling away a food supply; scrounging cans for kerosene storage; buying proper clothing and footgear; and cleaning the box stove and stove pipe for winter use.

Winter wasn't just another season in which you commented on the beauty of trees, or rearranged your sun reflector to even up your tan, or bemoaned the inconvenience of mud. Winter tested the ability to survive, to live through it. In winter, sometimes even breathing challenged the northerner.

Yet preparing for this winter involved much more than gathering and readying all the necessary props. For although I had lived in New England for nine years, this winter marked my first winter— my first winter in this cabin, in a New Hampshire woods, alone, without the usual linkages and couplings of an outside community. Yes, the winter cordwood, food, and water storage preoccupied my mind since May. But what really sent flickers of fear through my head was thoughts of long winter nights, perched here alone, snow and wind howling like a wild dog, the cabin and me literally, and figuratively, shaking.

I had struggled with woodchucks and mosquitoes and mice and stones and a whole spectrum of emotions, but I wondered if they only signaled skirmishes in a broader battle. Flickers of fear: as a full-length movie is actually a series of ordered flickers, each frame moving so quickly that all you see is a continuous image, so my fears and other emotions appeared to me. Life connected as one scenario, with frames made up of fears and hopes and laughter and tears and joys.

As my woods life shifted to winter, though, the filmstrip co-agulated and slowed down. I saw more frames, more parts of me.

I saw fewer ways of speeding up the film, like taking hikes and picking blueberries and going swimming. I saw me in a cabin with mirrors on opposite walls that translated as me seeing me seeing me ad infinitum.

Yes, to infinity. This would be my first infinite winter, for my insides really never ended.

# NOVEMBER

*November, with its rusty colors and dead leaves, proved a particularly hard month to live alone, so I unconsciously filled up my hours with more people: the food co-op, a weekly Backwoods Cabin radio show, volunteering at a local nursing home leading a music participation group, and periodically attending a Buddhist meditation gathering in town. My activity renewed an ancient process of huddling closer together as the season grew colder and windier.*

*I had also, for a brief time, gone back to psychotherapy in Boston, to deal with my ex-wife's death and the grieving that somehow came so hard for me. And the tears that surfaced during those sessions set the tone for the wet, cold days of November—tears that softened me to the hard weather ahead.*

I think when the universe big-banged into existence and all the months of all the seasons lined up to get their assignments and identities, November stood at the end of the line, protesting in a squeaky voice, "Hey, me too! Me too!" For me, November had always lacked something. At least, when rain and cold struck October, its great display of color soothed and warmed. But November had all the luster of an old rusty gate.

The cabin stayed warm with wood heat as a cold rain beat on bare branches of deciduous saplings. The thought of winter entered, the awesome winter, the first winter at this one-room cabin that was made originally to keep tools, not a human being, warm. Much preparation still lay ahead, a great flurry of activity still needed before the first snow rested its massive white hand, saying, "Be stiller now, Stephen. Walk more. Ski over the mountain to friends. Let that car rest now. Be more content with your own company. Plan your time in town carefully and economically."

But that snow was waiting for December. November's grayness and rust introduced a poor opening act to what lay ahead. The members of the audience held back their applause during this pre-winter month. Yet without November, would the first snow have been as beautiful a relief to the ubiquitous taupe? Would I have noticed the delicate patterns the ice made in my rain bucket? Would I have known that the wood I was cutting and hauling and splitting was more than just so many BTUs? Dour November made my wood-stove seem solar in its radiance.

In that light, this month of transition played an integral part in the cycles of the seasons and the cycles in me. One day I glanced up at an elephant-gray November sky, heavy with moisture, and noticed something I'd never seen before. It rivaled in excitement the first time I'd noticed leaves bursting from their flowers in spring.

*STEPHEN ALTSCHULER*

I saw buds, dormant, yet somehow bristling with a life force, braced against the sky like delicate yet tenacious webs. What was this? For years, I'd seen only the rusty drabness, the fallen leaves, the lackluster evergreens. I'd seen only the foreground of November, not its background. November did know life, hidden behind its cloak of brownish gray. Of course, it took my eyes, seeing, to pull back that cloak. How many times in the past had I looked up at November trees and seen only bareness, and at November skies and felt only cold, penetrating rain? I may not have known exactly where I was emotionally or how far I'd come in the six months I'd been there. But seeing those burnt sienna buds brightened the landscape some, putting me closer to the spirit of this late fall, just as water hauling, digging, gardening, berry picking, and hiking put me closer to my own nature.

More than anything, this time in the woods heightened my awareness of change. A time of discovery, of unfolding, then folding, then unfolding again. A time when the acknowledgement of fear, rather than leading to panic, germinated a seed of hope. This time in the woods enhanced my learning to trust—trust my insides, which were really the same as everything outside.

And now I could even trust my old nemesis, November. That didn't mean I liked the rusty hues and the bone-chilling rain, but I could count November as a beginning in a cycle of beginnings.

# FIRST SNOW

The cold, early December nights entered like bandits, making all of this part of New Hampshire hold its breath in anticipation. Looking forward to the first snow, hoping it would be a blizzard, I packed in supplies and provisions, using the old Rambler, which seemed to be happy in New Hampshire.

I drove the car too much that fall: too many errands, too many trips into Boston, too many nights out at the local folk-music cabaret. So I longed for the snows to keep me home and more inward, to help quiet a city-bred mind that seemed to always seek stimulation and diversion. I wondered if the car would be as happy with severe cold and snow, and with where I had to park—on a county-maintained forest road about a quarter mile from the cabin. Snowplows would probably bury me for the duration of the winter, and I would no longer have the privilege of choice.

But the first snow fell light and gentle, and I continued with my

*driving addiction, albeit more slowly on the slicker roads. That depend-*
*ence on the car was to change, with a jolt, on Christmas Eve. But for*
*now, all remained right with the world and the Rambler—tagged The*
*Rumbler by a mechanic friend—as winter painted its first sign of entry.*

As if nature had deftly waved a magic wand, the first snow came. One night, clear skies overhead; the next morning, all the ground white, not a trace of snow in the air. Like the wondrous childhood tooth fairy who somehow used to sneak in, leave her charm, and exit without a trace, the weather spirits cast their spell unnoticed.

I must have lain in bed an hour that morning looking out the long southern-exposed window of my sleeping loft, scanning the slope of the mountain made mystical by this frozen gift of the night. In earlier years I would have been scanning the radio for school or work cancellations. The consequence of snow was linked then to the whim of some school principal or boss who had the power to bring joy or disconsolation with his or her decision. My friends and I measured snow then as either good-for-nothing and not enough, which turned anticipatory joy quickly into sorrow, or fantastic and more-than-enough, which liberated me from being somewhere I'd rather not have been.

But here in this cabin, which more reflected my true self, the first snow was a harbinger. It, alone, was only the first snow of the season: nothing attached, no hopes or wishes or desires beyond it. But in my mind it was much more. The first snow harnessed a great positive force that helped me remember the sanctity of everyday life. I didn't even care or lament over the reason the three inches couldn't have been a foot. No regrets, this time, at this simple yet kaleidoscopic way-station on the road to Ixtlan. This new road I

*STEPHEN ALTSCHULER*

took was paved with hope even amid the occasional potholes. This snow, with its giant soothing fingers, massaged a brow that had been furrowed by the phalanx of city furies.

That first snow did more than soothe me spiritually, though. On a practical level, on the next night, it allowed me to do something I'd been afraid of doing before. Once the previous summer, after visiting a friend on the other side of the mountain, I set out after dark to walk home. The trek measured about a mile through wooded trails, and I had no flashlight. The night settled misty and very dark, and venturing into the woods I soon became disoriented. Ordinary branches loomed like specters, and the innocent creaks and cracks of the forest sounded ominous. Was that the trail? I think . . . no . . . maybe here . . . no. I couldn't handle the uncertainty, and my fantasies ran wild. I turned around and took the longer asphalt way home.

Six months later, on this night after the first snow, I again extended my visit past twilight and set out into the dark, forbidding woods—set out to again face shadows: of fear and uncertainty. This time, though, the spirits of snow had laid down a carpet of illumination. The trails didn't exactly glow, but the snow cover, even without a moon, had defined them enough to make them recognizable. Fears subsided as the unknown became more known, even though the only thing known was limited to that portion of trail the snow was immediately defining. No other landmarks pointed out the direction, only the ground under foot. Walking there felt like driving a car in dense fog, with only the dotted line on the road as a guide. That always took great concentration and faith that the line was drawn accurately. But sometimes, if the lines were not properly marked, I would head out into the fog, not knowing whether they would be there to guide the way.

Snow on the trail, though, and nature that created it, never disappointed me, and walking home that night, I felt the first snow as a thread connecting me to the earth—a hemline thread, really, that would one day disappear, leaving me on my own to find my way. Like a great spiritual teacher the snow gave itself completely to the moment, offering the example of its own life. It did not teach: it allowed learning. It did not speak of the truth: it showed the truth. It showed the way home without intending to show the way home. In fact, this first snow intended nothing at all and had no purpose other than to be the first snow. Great teachers were like that as well. They didn't teach: they just lived their lives fully for all to see.

The first snow was just being itself on the trail, giving anyone the opportunity to use it to his or her advantage. I was there following it—just following—until it led me to my backwoods haven. If I could live like that, trusting and seeing the truth before me, being open to all the possibilities and opportunities, all the remaining snows of the rest of my life—indeed, all the remaining moments of life—would be as first snows, as child snows, as beginner snows allowing perpetual discovery of life's wonder and wisdom.

# STORM

The first storm of the season blew in on Christmas Eve. I remember that date because the next day—Christmas Day—I discovered that The Rumbler had been ignominiously vandalized and, given my limited income, made inoperable.

I'd been working on the car's water pump the whole day of Christmas Eve—a hopeless venture that my ego would not let go of until common sense and waning daylight finally got me to stop. I returned to the cabin about a quarter-mile away to await the arrival of the expected storm. Stoking the stove, I sat back in my oak swivel chair, thought (and worried a bit) about what not having a car through the winter would be like, filled my favorite pipe, and watched the first snowflakes arrive, gently at first, then heavier as the northeast wind started to kick up like a snorting bull, as it does when it readies itself for a hard blow.

As the night and storm progressed I wrote in my journal: "A bliz-

*zard rages outside. Such storms fulfill dreams. They help make sense of
all the fear and insanity. I am part of the storm, holed up here in this
cabin—so close to it—the wind, the cold, the intense blowing snow.
What am I? What am I doing on this earth? Just this—just watching
a storm rage in a tick of time."*

The first significant weather served up an early taste of what
was to come, for the storm that stomped through qualified as a real
bona fide winter event, complete with raging winds, severe cold,
and snow that blew and swirled its way into every crevice of the
woodpile. "Snow changing to rain, with temperatures in the twenties," the myopic weather service reported. Even an amateur weather
buff like me knew that water vapor in the twenties had to be frozen.

Like most storms, this one started gently enough—a few scout
flakes sent down to reconnoiter the ground for stick-ability. It seems
everything checked out, because soon after, the wind picked up,
and tree limbs, branches, and twigs responded like nerve ganglia
braced for danger.

And my ganglia bristled as well. Was I ready? All the preparation, the wood gathering, the food storage, the winter provisions,
the kerosene stockpile, the woodstove, the protective clothing, and,
of course, my mental state, would now be tested. A trip into town
that day . . . let's see . . . better get some canned goods and bread.
What else? I flitted about like a squirrel from store to store, knowing,
just knowing, I'd forgotten something.

But yes, finally, ultimately, I was ready; if the snow piled so
high that I couldn't open my door, I would survive. In fact, I kind
of wished it would. Being snowbound was a childhood dream. I
could never get enough snow. And Philadelphia winters just didn't
fully satisfy my cravings. I dreamed of living in a place where winters

*STEPHEN ALTSCHULER*

would always be white—no rain, just snow upon snow upon snow. Even after I aged a bit and joined the rest of the automobile fanatics and stalled and discharged and skidded on winter roads turned into ghostly auto graveyards, I still loved snow and all its wonder and drama and fun.

But never had I been so close to a storm as now. Never were life supports so dependent on my own doing. And never have I enjoyed a winter storm as much. With my stove stoked to capacity, kerosene lamps glowing with special softness and radiance, I sat back in the silence of my cabin, waiting, listening.

First, gentle flakes in the fading late afternoon light—familiar, steady, contained, not yet a full storm, waiting for the cloak of night to unleash its full fury. And here in the woods, night is truly night—no street or car lights to define the intensity of the storm, to add the visual to the auditory and make it less forbidding.

As the dark descended, the wind and driving snow began to pelt the cabin with a vengeance. The structure shook with each gust, a shaking that momentarily paralleled my own as I imagined the roof flying off or the walls collapsing. But the dwelling held intact, and a point came when I knew I'd make it through.

I knew then I'd survive the winter.

Although I'd continue to stumble and grope through my learning of this woods life—although my mind would continue to snag on the barbs at its edges—I was prepared enough inside not only to weather the fierce winter storms but to enjoy them in the solitude and magic of my cabin.

I made myself a nice dinner that night, sipped a good wine, reflected on childhood winters of shooting hills with a Flexible Flyer. And for that moment, during that storm, I had a feeling of fulfillment. It didn't last long because I was still enmeshed in the cobwebs of what fulfillment and success are supposed to be. I was still enmeshed, too, in the fallout of past phobias and traumas, like my ex-wife's death, which still felt as if a wall inside me had collapsed.

But for that moment, my mind cleared of the past, contentment and joy filled me, and that storm and the cabin and the woods fit me like a well-worn shoe. For that moment I caught a glimpse of what was real about life, separated from the ideas of it I had created through conditioned thought.

But then, the fire was getting low . . . and I went out to get more wood . . . which was all wet and snow-covered . . . since I hadn't protected it enough . . . and my castle of contentment started to crumble. The storm seemed to pause as a hurricane does when the eye passes overhead. Just then I caught sight of a flash of headlight coming from the road where my car was parked dead, and I wondered who would be out driving Timbertop Road on such a night—and Christmas Eve, no less. I shrugged and remembered, "Christmas Eve. It's Christmas Eve," and went back inside, poured more wine, and toasted all that was good and at peace on Earth.

*STEPHEN ALTSCHULER*

# 13

# WINTER NIGHT SKY

    *I experienced more storms—snow and rain and those inside me. I was spending much more time in the cabin now, having fewer visits with friends. I took time to look up more at the stars against a bootblack sky and discover a world previously blocked out by the city, a night-sky world that drew my eye into an awesome realization of the possibility that none of this had an end. The perception took my breath away for a moment, and a bolt of anxiety rippled through my head. I imagined the cosmic explosion that some say started it all as I stood, shivering, on a small piece of ground, covered with snow, in a forest in southwestern New Hampshire on the planet Earth looking up and out at a sky that sparkled like a manifestation—if I could only realize it—of my own being.*

For a short time, when the moon was nearing its full phase, its reflection on the ice-crusted trees and snow made my cabin seem more a palace than a primitive woodland dwelling. The winter night sky and landscape framed my place as if it were a fine work of art and heightened for me the realities of aloneness and independence. And during the stove-black sky of the new moon, those feelings were even more intense. The vastness of that sky: Where did it end? Where did it begin? Nowhere to nowhere? The possibility made me dizzy with awe . . . and fear.

For if the universe was infinite and was the sum total of all its parts, then all its parts were infinite: you, I, plants, trees, woodchucks, hawks, were all integral parts of the universe and so must be infinite as well. When I sat alone or snowshoed through the winter night, I sometimes thought about these things and longed to be rooted. For the awesomeness and vastness of the universe was staggering and made me want to hug the earth as we all hurtled through limitless space. Trees were rooted to the soil, soil to rocks, rocks to the earth's core, and the core, the planet itself, to the sun.

But what about me, the wanderer who had sojourned from city alleys to small-town lanes to backwoods trails, who had been through a burned-out marriage and more dead-end relationships than I cared to think about, who had struggled with those inner parts that felt both like a bobbing balloon on a string and a necklace beaded with heavy lead weights? Was this cabin just another way station? Another pit stop on the path toward my inner self? When would I arrive? Or was the journey like the deep endless winter sky with a periodic full moon to illuminate the way and make the trees dance? I really didn't know—which is an answer a certain Zen Master I knew would smile at, and say, "Go straight ahead. Only keep this 'don't know' mind."

*STEPHEN ALTSCHULER*

# 14 HEATING WITH WOOD

By mid-January my physical isolation had deepened. Emotionally, a depression set in. The usual ways I'd bolstered my ego in the past were less available to me in the country. My sources of self-esteem had to be redefined, since I had no job or relationship or much contact with people. And all this was heightened in a season when the whole universe seemed to inhale and hibernate.

I'd taken on a greater risk, living in the woods—not so much external but internal. I'd chopped off a few more exits. And as I aged there was less margin for error. This made me more frightened of the moment—frightened of seeing who I really was under the layers that years of therapy were unable to peel off. I suspected that inside me lived a passionate, expressive, exuberant man. But I feared the moment that contained it all—that less-than-a-tick-in-time moment I'd labored to know and experience but that eluded me.

Needing to heat my place by my own devices was a saving grace of sorts. Not only did it keep me warm, it kept me busy, something that on emotional levels was just as important as the physical heat. It created a sense of purpose I had lost momentarily, along with my references to the outside world. It got my mind off myself for the time being—got me out of the cabin and its walls of figurative mirrors.

Through the simple act of wood-gathering, splitting, and burning, I began to regain that appreciation for the moment and my capacity to experience it with senses and a spirit numbed by years of neglect.

Like water that had its origins in pure, wild mountain streams or nascent underground springs, wood, too, came from a wondrous place. It came from the creek-y, filigreed, mossy, mystical, yet absolutely real world of woodland. In my former world of pre-packaged convenience, even wood—firewood—showed up neatly piled on a truck, cut to proper length, sometimes even split—I'd even heard of it wrapped in plastic with a carrying handle—ready to be tossed into urban woodstoves that were becoming more and more high-tech.

I came across an amazing statistic, one that placed me and my environs more in New England's majority. It was that eighty-seven percent of New Hampshire is woodland. And the figure for the other two northern New England states was similar. That meant that all the concrete, golden-arched, power-lined, parking-lot other stuff—the thirteen percent that got all the attention and press—was really just an anomaly in the domain of wood.

During mid-winter days I was intimate with that woodland majority, spending much of my time hauling hardwood, cut by a former owner of this land and seasoned and streaked with weather and wind and age—seasoned like a sharp old Yankee, who matured and ripened with each cycle of seasons.

It was hard work for a guy who was born into the oil age, but hauling wood from the forest to my place became a part of my cycle. It put that wood—its full weight, coarse texture, tawny hues, alive aromas—closer to me. It involved me fully in a process that preserved my life with warmth.

Staying warm with wood formed the cornerstone of winter conversation between my neighbors and me. Everyone had a different method, a different formula, a different wood heater, and a different harrowing story to tell about the way he or she teetered on the edge of Arctic oblivion.

For me, heating with wood became an art form and I a fledgling artist. And like forms of art, the results were commensurate with knowing the fundamentals and then applying them over and over until the rote performance flowed naturally into newness, creativity, and serendipity. Yes, wood heat, at least from my perspective, could be creative.

Heating with wood involved many variables to adjust and experiment with—the type and age of the wood, its length and the way it was positioned in the stove, and the woodstove itself and the spot where it was situated. And then there were the finer points, too—the kindling, the amount of paper to start the fire, and the most enigmatic factor of all: banking, manipulating, and coaxing the fire to last through the night, thus easing the chore of the ritual morning fire-starting . . . and starting of myself.

One of the real satisfactions of living at the cabin in winter was that staying warm depended entirely on my own doing. Of course, if my doing was a bit haphazard, then staying warm became a kind of constant hovering over the woodstove, as if hugging it and nursing from it.

It was like that in December during a cold spell. In the summer I'd bought an old-fashioned cast-iron box stove and figured that it would be just right for my small space. In buying this stove I walked one of those fine lines between Yankee thrift and just being cheap about the whole thing. Well, it worked out great when the temperature was forty—in fact, a little too well at times, when the inside became hotter than the outside—but when the temperature plunged to minus fifteen, the stove seemed to get more crotchety and cantankerous. I'd have to sleep next to it and get up every two hours and feed the little stoveling. My woodpile was dwindling rapidly, and I was dwindling rapidly; my energy level compared with that of a new parent with an infant to tend constantly.

So I finally broke down before I broke down literally and bought a good air-tight wood burner. It was still an art form, using this new stove—the tricks of efficient starting, stoking it with enough and the right combination of hard and soft wood . . . to get that extra hour of hot coals . . . and sleep. And as long as it remains an art form, wood heat probably won't be used by the majority. But when using wood heat becomes as easy as adjusting a thermostat, and the newer models continue to reduce wood's particulate pollutants, then the Arabs had better start budgeting their oil-generated billions.

Energy independence: This country certainly has the technology and expertise to achieve it. And I agree with some astute observers that technology needn't be an antagonist. It can be used to develop clean energy sources. Technology can work in harmony with nature, allowing use of its resources in a sane, efficient way.

Wood heat warmed me from the inside and gave me a satisfying sense of control over one of the basics of survival in the North. Such heat came from the trees that grew close by—beech, birch, maple, and pine—and my wood stove retained an element of mystery and challenge in staying warm within a small but significant corner of that eighty-seven percent of wood wonderland.

*STEPHEN ALTSCHULER*

# THE SILENCE

In the dormancy of winter, particularly winter nights, I reflected on the way my mind could still be noisy in the midst of such total silence. But, after thirty-some years of living in cities, I was quieter than when I first moved into the cabin—a quiet nurtured by the stillness of the woods.

A quiet, too, that came with feeling more in control of my life—less fearful, in better physical shape, less attached to excesses of food, tobacco, and entertainment. I felt more content with simple activities than I had been in the city, more content with less stimuli. This became ever clearer after a mid-winter trip to visit friends in Boston allowed close comparison of my states of mind in these two seemingly opposite places. What I saw drew me closer to the cabin.

I'd been in Boston for several days and returned like a weary pilgrim, gone too long from home. I'd survived a tumultuous time, a time filled with much emotional and physical noise in that world away from the cabin in the woods. At times I felt off balance, off-centered in that world of speeding cars and neon signs and blaring music and inflated talking—things that made it difficult to keep hold of myself.

When I returned and settled once again into this cabin and the woods, I was greeted by a healer of sorts. I think the quiet, the silence of the woods, an almost rhythmic silence, cradled my head and stroked my temples—a silence that enveloped and held me tight the way a loving mother does, a silence that cleared away the rubble, that let me see me seeing me. Once, at 3:00 A.M., I awoke to the sound of a Great Horned Owl giving its haunting call, and my whole being felt clear and open as I listened. I'd discovered a middle-of-the-night mind:

> Sometimes in the middle of the night
> I awake and see it all so clearly:
> the joy, the peace, the pain,
> arranged in simple harmony,
> a steady summer rain.

> Sometimes in the middle of the night
> I quiver with discovery
> that all the rubble has its place
> And all it needs is a middle-of-the-night mind
> to find the space.

The silence scared me when I first moved here. Where were all the familiar cues? Where were the cacophonous machines and

*STEPHEN ALTSCHULER*

appliances that kept me from feeling too lonely? Where were all the words that shrouded my insides with smog? Here I heard gentle sounds, not apart from life but a part of it. As one of my mentors, Alan Watts, said all along: Out here, the verb wasn't separate from the noun. When a tree creaked, it manifested treeing: being a tree. When a bird chirped, it expressed birding: just going about the business of being a bird. The sounds of the woods defined the beings making them. No antagonism existed between the sound and the environment, as with a car or a TV or an over-worded voice. And without that antagonism arose more peace. More middle-of-the-night mindedness.

The silence didn't frighten me any more. In fact, every day I immersed myself in it through Zen meditation, which helped quiet me, putting me more in touch with my real depths and permitting a wider view of all life outside myself—more in touch with the breathing that sustained me and the breathing that sustained the woods.

Then in those fleeting, ephemeral moments when I could silence my thinking mind I got into a kind of eternal boat and flowed down a lazy river. I forgot my self for a time, and in the forgetting, found my real self—found it among chipmunk-ing and owl-ing and tree-ing and wind-ing. I just settled into the silence, and breathed, and began Stephen-ing.

# SNOWSHOEING

In winter, nothing grew but silence, which I helped maintain by not owning anything motorized. I got around on cross-country skis, and I remember my first time using them: about the only thing I did right was walk uphill. I eventually became proficient enough with Nordic skiing to teach the sport to beginners (true chutzpa after only a year of being on them myself!), but snowshoes—the old-fashioned kind made of wood and rawhide—held more fascination for me. So one of the first things I did when I moved in during the spring was to buy a pair at a local flea market.

The thought of winter's excesses rattled me at times, bringing up shadows and insecurities. But sitting in my place and imagining myself *on snowshoes somehow helped me cope with the Furies of the mind. And when it came time to use them, I found the act even better than the thought of it.*

Snowshoes represented a basic ingredient of life in the winter woods. They allowed the fetching and lugging home of water as well as climbing the mountain for wood-hunting expeditions in knee-deep snow. But more than that, they fulfilled a long-time fantasy. For years while living in cities I'd imagine myself snowshoeing through the woods, exploring, immersing myself in the silence, devoid of droning cars and trucks—a feeling approaching unity with the woods. And for years I longed for that fantasy to become reality, but somehow it was always thwarted. That frustrated longing seemed to parallel my non-readiness for living away from the city.

So on moving to the woods one of the first things I bought was a pair of snowshoes, despite the fact it was only May. Admonitions about New Hampshire winters somehow made May seem just the right time to get prepared.

It was after the first three-inch snowfall—that's right, a mere three inches—that the snowshoes saw their first duty as I went trudging about, being careful to avoid the pebbles that were still exposed. I had a fine time until the tip of one snowshoe found its way to the tail of the other, and, alas, came the discovery of the quintessence of a true klutz.

But I got up and squared my snowshoes and waddled back to my cabin, then hung them on the wall and admired them a bit, old and weathered wood, rough-hewn rawhide, hard saddle leather bindings—a harmony of grain and amber hue, like the dream of

*STEPHEN ALTSCHULER*

them I once pictured. Dreams and fantasies fulfilled. It didn't happen often, but when it did, feelings of newness and excitement and hope rushed in—that child's rush of waking to the first heavy snow of the winter.

I felt a certain sadness when dreams came true, too, because then the dream was lost and the initial joy could easily seem monotone by the repetition of reality. Keeping hold of the quality of the dream, of the fantasy, after it became reality required skillful awareness. It required what the late Zen Master Shunryu Suzuki Roshi called "beginner's mind," which referred to the mind that existed before conceptual thinking separated the observer from the observed. It paralleled an infant's mind, unburdened by conditioning but with the consciousness and wisdom of an adult who has seen and felt the suffering of life and has decided to stay alive and help. Beginner's mind embodied both the practical and the dreamy—like wearing those snowshoes.

I used my snowshoes almost every day that winter. The newness wore off, and wearing them became as commonplace as slipping into a faithful and comfortable pair of boots. And although I no longer spent long periods of time meditating on the twinning of the rawhide webbing, I still dreamed and anticipated adventures on my snowshoes, like the first day I walked to the other side of the mountain—about a mile of wooded trails—and walked back the same night in the moonlight, pausing often to hear the silence around me. And my expeditions up and around the mountain in search of a day's supply of hardwood. Or the misty image of that huge, old, seasoned white oak—deadwood, standing somewhere in waiting, ready to serve and warm the first ambitious soul whose bushwhacking trek has been determined and persistent enough. My trusty snowshoes would take me to that oak and to . . . who knew what treasures of the winter woods beyond?

For as the newness of life in the woods matured, I still dreamed. And although the dream sometimes got muted by the din of the mundane and the chatter of my thinking mind, I knew, as with my snowshoeing dream during those years in the city, that everything that happened, even the most seemingly insignificant happening, contained part of the dream. I just needed to keep dreaming and living and snowshoeing up the mountain looking for wood.

*STEPHEN ALTSCHULER*

# 17 MARCH

With the approaching vernal equinox and the official start of spring, this sort-of-young man's fancy turned toward a woman I met at a friend's party. Cabin fever, or the tendency to climb the walls near the end of winter, was rising. Being a bit out of romantic practice, I found my powers of social discrimination weak, though. My spring fancy was as unstable as the weather, she not being particularly healthy and I still crusty from an isolated winter and still-fresh memories of my ex-wife's suicide.

Emotions around this relationship went up and down, affected by past wounds and the present vicissitudes of this wildly fickle month. March was unsettling. The relationship did not last long past the equinox. But simple attention to the details of nature, as always, helped me keep in sight both my center and my life's destination and purpose, which was to live skillfully and mindfully each step of the journey.

With the coming of March, my mind languished either in the future, dreaming of blossoming leaves and shoots of peas and wild trillium on the woodland floor, or in the past, licking my wounds of the winter and marveling that I made it through in pretty good shape. March epitomized such thinking. In fact, it wouldn't surprise me if Julius Caesar got so caught up in the reveries of spring that he thought Brutus was coming by to borrow a cup of sugar.

So instead of being *beware* of the Ides of March, I tried to be *aware* of March's subtle yet wondrous transitions. As November cowered at the gateway of the long, droning winter—a kind of Charon at the river Styx—March mirrored Icarus, rising high toward the spring sun, too confident, until its waxed wings melted and it plummeted to earth as a fresh winter storm or cold spell—a plunge that caught me and my wood supply off guard. "I've got more than enough wood," I said to myself at the beginning of the month. But each day of sub-freezing, windswept, and sometimes snowy weather withered my pile dangerously low.

In New Hampshire, folks branded March a winter month, yet the lifeblood of spring began to flow. As the days warmed, the maple sap rose in the awakening trees. The snow cover, which seemed as if it would last until June, began to recede—slow, recalcitrant. A day with the temperature in the fifties, the next, winter again—a storm, a cold penetrating wind, made even colder by the brief offerings of warmth and the way it tricked the mind into complacence. Yet the signs accented the coming change—the longer days, the copious flow of maple sap, and the way that sap turned milky when the buds were pregnant with leaf blossoms.

The forest seemed to bristle with more activity. Small animals, as evidenced by their tracks, crisscrossed, like busy shoppers, from tree to tree. More birds paused from their intense business of winter

*STEPHEN ALTSCHULER*

survival to sing a few notes of springtime exultation. March was the herald of salvation for the forest. All around, trees stood winter-weary, rocked and buffeted and battered by the three Furies: December, January, and February.

Some trees were down and gone, sacrifices to the nature spirits. Others stood scarred and limbless, creaking "Waltzing Matilda" as the cold March winds bullied them, emulating the power of January—a power forever denied March by the higher and longer course of the sun. The equinox neared, and the thought of it sustained me through this ephemeral late winter. For, like the trees, my veneer had been worn thin by violent winter winds and weather.

Yet also like the majority of trees, my core was intact and strengthened by this winter experienced and survived. I emerged from the battle triumphant and, in the struggling, knew more of me—my resilience, my fears, my capacities, my failings. Yet, as my internal conflict of opposites continued, March lingered incomplete, unfinished, a Panmunjom among months. Love, hate; open, closed; sadness, joy; heart, head; fear, peace—opposites that March reflected.

For like no other month, March signaled an end and a beginning. It was the death of winter and the conception of spring. It was a depleted woodpile and a plan for the garden. In March thoughts turned away from the tempered-steel winter toward the butterfly spring. Yet March bent like an apple branch, springy and whippy, then snapped—an exaggerated blast of cold and storm if you let your mind get too far ahead.

But on the ends of the windblown branches of this wild month, buds clung poised and ready to pirouette when the curtain rose. And with March, the crowd stirred and the show began.

# THE SNOW COVER

With the ending of my brief romantic relationship, cabin fever grew to dangerous levels. The crusty, increasingly dirty snow cover didn't help matters. And skiing or snowshoeing weren't much fun any more. I tried tapping maple trees but got only about a gallon for two weeks' work (although it was the tastiest gallon of liquid I'd ever drunk).

So I kept my sights outward and finally connected with another woman, someone I'd known as a friend, and the connection now crossed the fault line into something deeper. And despite some basic differences— she was more city, I was more country—our hearts resided in similar places.

We continued for a while, and I almost forgot about the lingering *winter, but eventually this budding relationship, like the last, failed to germinate and grow.*

*As it does every year, the ice finally melted on the ponds and lakes. The snow cover, at least on the south- and west-facing slopes, receded. And my cabin fever broke with the first elixir-like smells of spring, damp and green.*

Like a visitor who came for the weekend and stayed several weeks, the snow cover was in March at the limits of its welcome. For the most part the snow had been a friend and companion during the long winter. It had been a cushion to settle into, something whose contours I could meld with. For here in the woods the snow maintained its pristine magic—a magic sculpted deftly into a Rodin woman by wind and weather. No plows or exhaust fumes or road salt denigrated its delicate crystals. No forces, save nature, tugged at its grip—a caressing grip—on the dormant forest floor. It was a wonder of winter, this snow cover.

Yet in late March the snow cover croaked like the lone crotchety "Nay" at town meeting after a thunderous chorus of "ayes." Just about everyone I spoke to then concurred: they were tired of it. They'd had it up to their ears . . . and front doors . . . and were even ready and looking forward to mud, that delinquent child of the melting snow.

Even a hard-core snow lover like me was ready for its final demise. I never thought I'd hear myself admit that, for my feeling for snow went very deep—back to the roots of childhood sledding on city streets and to wide-eyed excitement watching TV weathermen as they warned of imminent winter storms. But there, at the cabin, the snow was more than a recreational whim, more than a means to miss work or school on a Monday morning. It was an intimate part of my life, as if we'd been living together for the past four months. And anytime I lived so closely with another entity, I needed periodic space to gather myself together, to reaffirm that the universe was constantly in flux and changing. Four months together, and I began forgetting that the snow was the snow and I was I. I started fantasizing that I was melting when too near the wood stove.

I made it through that winter without contracting a serious case of cabin fever but could almost taste sweet spring, a taste diluted by the lingering snow cover as water diluted the sweetness of running maple sap. I wished the snow could leave instantly—vanish and soak completely into the soil so that the earth that was concrete-covered would not be flooded. For there arose a certain pain and sadness in seeing this ace starter slink off the mound toward the dugout, knocked about by a slew of cheap singles.

The snow, once so noble and solid in its power, secure that the sun was too low and short-lived to erode its empire, now lay less confident. Its heyday had peaked as it huffed winter's last breath—the final vestige of its severe physiognomy, which now showed more and more the rough-hewn signs of age, the glazed ice of night, and the soggy slush of days.

I felt sad at this death of winter. Yet, as my body adjusted to the subtle transitions, I felt more energy flowing. For the lifeblood of the forest was rising, and with the completion of this first woodland winter, I'd been baptized into its fellowship. And as part of that baptism I had learned more vividly than ever that death spawned life, winter the spring, and the gently receding snow cover the ascending wonder of rebirth and renewal in the natural environment.

# THE KITTENS

My two short-lived relationships with women brought me to an acknowledgement that I didn't feel ready for a full-blown primary relationship and perhaps never would. So I made a new commitment to myself and settled back into more solitary living. The warmer weather, and prospects of its getting even warmer, helped me renew the feeling I had the previous year when I moved in.

My cats and I returned to better terms, too, since they were more agreeable now about being outdoor cats. In fact, they preferred the outdoors, with all the springtime critters they could stalk there. And I would watch them for hours, a sort of backwoods version of a couch potato, but this watching wasn't so passive because it led to some valuable insights on the way life could be lived. They didn't know it, but those cats were my teachers, and I loved coming to class.

For I didn't live totally alone in that cabin. I had two cabin-mates, whom I was very close to and loved a lot. Their names were Karma and Dharma (Sanskrit words loosely meaning "destiny" and "the laws of nature," respectively). But let me introduce them to you with a poem/song I composed about them early one spring day as they "attacked" each other, their tantalizing tails baiting, goading, and twitching.

### Kittens on the Roam

I've got a couple of muffins,
A couple of tiger cats.
Fluffy as a powder puffin'.
Quicker than an old barn bat.
They love to go a-stalkin'
in the high grass round my home,
a walkin' and a pawkin',
fierce lions on the roam.

First they see a dragonfly,
then another, then another.
They're so confused as they all fly by
that they pounce on each other.
They roll and play and chase their tails
till they're all tired out.
Like a fading wind that leaves their sails,
they purr a sleepy pout.

And then they're off a-dreamin'
in a field in early morn.

And what's growin' there and steamin'
are melted butter and kettles of corn.

Now they're up and stretchin',
they look around with cobweb eyes.
Then they're off fun-fetchin',
no if, ands, buts, or whys.
First they see a ball of string,
then they go watch dripping water.
To them the world's a big plaything,
and I think that's how it oughter . . . be

cause my little kittens are totally alive.
They don't need Zen Buddhist sittin's.
They don't want, worry, or strive.
Just give them both a bowl of food
and a nice warm lap to sit in.
And they'll be in a happy mood,
my two contented kittens.

Now, these guys weren't as innocent as the ditty suggests. In
fact, shortly after I wrote it they killed and devoured six mice, a
mole, a bird, and a snake. And if you've ever seen a cat feasting on
a little critter, you know these domesticated cuties still have a lot
of their wild ancestors in them.

One friend of mine even suggested that because of this wanton
carnage, cats shouldn't live as pets in the woods. I replied that if
you went by that reasoning I, or any of us, shouldn't be living there
either, with the mosquito- and mice-killing of my own.

But really, neither was right. The kittens and I hadn't exactly
joined the backwoods Mafia. Little Karma never came up to me
saying, "Meyah, all right, Backwoods Stephen, I'm Kitty-faced
Karma, the hit kitten from Chicago, Meyah. Who's the mark today?"

No, the kittens and I remained part of the woods, the kittens being farther along in the flow of nature than I, since they reacted so spontaneously to everything. We all took our chances living there. The kittens could fall prey to a swooping hawk, or get killed by a raccoon or lanced by a porcupine. And I was subject to wild animals, storms, and tricks my mind could play on me.

All of which helped me stay less attached to my cats, less attached because things were always changing in the woods—and everywhere, for that matter—so I could lose any possession in a moment. A lot of potential pain and suffering could come if I clung onto things—even things or people or pets I loved.

Recently, on the night of the full moon, Karma, herself barely out of kittenhood, gave birth to a litter of squealing, writhing kittens. In fact, she chose my bed at 2:00 A.M. to perform this most commonplace of miracles, so I had a close-up view of all the participants. How exciting and awesome that first breath must be, and the inherent courage to take it! Yet if death came in the next moment—and I feared it would, because she chose a spot near the edge of the sleeping loft—they would take it as they did their first breath: as it came.

Maybe it was that simple—air comes and breathing begins; air goes and breathing stops. No difference. No duality. No birth. No death. No beginning. No end. These kittens were not experiencing a beginning: they *were* the beginning, they *were* the breath. Verb and noun were one and the same.

So I would continue to try to live like my cats: to take life as it came moment after moment, to breathe from my belly and live it to the fullest. Beyond that—theories be damned—who knows?

STEPHEN ALTSCHULER

# SHELTER

*With the winter well past and spring busting out, I remembered that May marked my first anniversary at the cabin. I sat back and marveled at the way my view of it, and me in it, had changed from when I first moved in. In fact, the original tenant, a young man, built it as a tool shed, and tools at first seemed more appropriate for the building than to have me living there. I looked over the inside. Obviously, not a lot of care had gone into making things straight and square. Good, I thought, for nature grew not particularly straight and square, and since I lived more in conjunction with nature, a wiggly place fit right in.*

*It had gotten larger, this cabin, not in actual size but in the way I perceived it. When I first saw it the winter before the move and traversed its length in about three steps, it simply seemed too small. It compared to the size of a cell in the state prison I worked at a few years before, yet this was no prison cell. And from the time I moved in, my universe, including this space-capsule cabin, began to expand.*

*On my anniversary night I played my guitar and sang and thanked the spirit guides for bringing me to that place. I felt centered, and I acknowledged that the conveniences of that other life were not particularly necessary, that I had all the light, food, heat, and water I needed. With my tiny cabin decorated simply and functionally, I felt comfortable. And with the night sky and the Milky Way for a canopy, I felt alive and free. I felt alive and free.*

By chance, I discovered a couple of neighborhood homes this spring, about the finest homes, all around, I've seen in this region. They looked energy efficient, had solid foundations, and possessed an architecture that blended with the environment so completely, that if I hadn't seen the residents enter, I would never have known they existed. Furthermore, the residents paid no property taxes, had no lawns to keep up, and put as much maintenance into them as you would into a hole in the ground. In fact, they *were* holes in the ground.

One appeared like a rather attractive open-portico design owned by a waddling woodchuck—I presumed widowed, divorced, or deserted, since she lived only with a small kit. A minuscule mole occupied the other, and judging from the way she carried her young one around by the nape of the neck whenever she left the hole, she struggled with that whole independence/dependence issue.

Whatever their personal situations, these creatures built absolutely revolutionary dwellings. No mortgage, no monthly utility payments, no aluminum siding, no paint, no concrete pavement/parking lot-induced flooded cellars.

No, we needn't live like woodchucks and moles. Extremes of

any kind can lead to trouble. But humans have gone to the extreme in the opposite direction. I walked around the area I lived in, and conspicuous, overbuilt houses found me, not the other way around. I saw foundations bulldozed and blasted out of virgin forest floor, boulders thrown up against trees and delicate plant life, whole tracts denuded of vegetation and subdivided and numbered and parceled out and sold like African slaves at a Maryland market. Builders placed houses in opposition to, and with protection from, the environment, set apart from it like adversaries in a courtroom. And their disputes with it came not necessarily from the home owners themselves but from banks, realtors, and the viccisitudes of the marketplace. Many conservatives railed about too much government control and regulation, but some of our most conservative citizens, bankers, laid down such a set of rules about the way houses must be built that homes wound up looking like those of Malvina Reynolds's song, "Little boxes on the hillside, little boxes made of ticky tacky."

If I had gone into a bank to apply for a mortgage on building a cabin like mine, I would have been laughed right out of the place. That is, I would have been suggested out of the bank with odd stares from those who looked askance. No resale value. No road frontage. No conventional septic system. Bankers might have said something like, "I'm sorry, sir, but the fact that the—ahem—outhouse is built into the structure does not mitigate the other negative conditions."

My dwelling may not have had these amenities, but it stayed cool in hot weather and warm in winter, put little strain on the surrounding environment, and put me closer to the earth, closer to my roots. A simple place fulfilling simple needs, yet it did much more than shield me from the elements. It linked me with nature just as surely as city apartments separated me from it. It felt like an extension of myself, part of a definition of myself, much the same as the woodchuck's den defined an integral part of the woodchuck. The dweller, the dwelling, and the earth dwelled upon intertwined as one strong cord.

The man who built that woodland shelter wasn't much on square windows and doors, but he built a place that grew out of the hillside the way the red maple trees around it did. Like most human dwellings, my place, too, was a refuge, a kind of decompression chamber to retreat to after bouts with the sometimes chaotic and nerve-jangling work-a-day world. But it also represented an affirmation of my position in nature. The cabin served as a reminder that I wasn't made from, nor will I return to, asphalt and aluminum siding and plastic golden arches. It stood as an affirmation of chirping birds and purring cats and breezes through trees. It affirmed that simple things really were simple and could once again be.

# BLUEBERRY PICKIN'

*With the second summer I began to lose my clarity, my sense of purpose as to what exactly I was doing living in the country— what I was doing with my life. The woods felt like a relay station between the material world and the monastic path, and I wondered if I fooled myself by trying to play both sides. I felt calmer, more centered, but I still suffered a great deal from old emotional pains. I wondered if living there suggested just avoiding more disappointment in the material world. Maybe I merely sought a safe haven.*

*I found my answers that summer in simple activities, activities that made the questions moot, activities like walking, hiking, and climbing, which in July led inevitably to another act of rather divine simplicity: finding blueberries. Picking them lightened my spirit—got me more at-*

*tuned with the earth and sky and natural processes of food-gathering that had been an integral part of human life until relatively recently.*

One thing I always planned to learn more about, while living in the country, was wild foods. Mostly, that plan stayed at the fantasy stage: I perused my wild-foods handbook and occasionally glanced out the window checking out all that supposedly succulent greenery. Somehow, though, I couldn't get interested in some of the things in that book, like poke and milkweed and cattails. I guess with my city upbringing even wild foods needed to have a touch of convenience in them—not exactly pre-packaged, plastic-wrapped, or oven-ready, but a shade easier than pouring off three boilings of milkweed pods before they were edible.

My idea of the perfect wild food was the berry. Particularly the blueberry, the most ubiquitous of all berries in southwestern New Hampshire. Blueberries were easily identified, even easier to pick, and came all natural and ready to eat, with absolutely no preservatives or additives.

I launched into some serious blueberry picking that summer. My friends and I debated and discussed the best ways to preserve and cook these precious blue jewels—anything from drying to freezing to making jam. But the best way I found, the one perfected by the black bear, involved the following technique: plotz down on your haunches and start yanking those berries as if you were working a cow's udders. Any container would do, but the best one I found also qualified as the most natural: my mouth.

Let me explain my method a bit further with a poem/song I composed at the top of Barrett Mountain one fine, clear day in July during a lull in the blueberry milking.

STEPHEN ALTSCHULER

## Blueberry Pickin'

Blueberry Pickin', all I want to do,
Is a pick 'em and eat 'em
My whole life through.

You don't need much equipment,
And you can even be dumb.
Because all you need to pick 'em
Is some fingers and a thumb.

And if you ain't got a thumb, my friend,
Then pick 'em with your toes.
And if you ain't got them either,
Then pick 'em with your nose.

If your nose is stuffed up,
Tell you what you can do.
Get down on your hands and knees
And chew, people, chew.

And if you run out of berries,
And that can happen I suppose,
Then go ask the governor,
Where blueberries grow.
(But I doubt if he knows.)

Wild, sweet, free food. So why the struggle with that wood-chuck who continued to munch on my garden if I could get all the vegetables and fruit I needed right there in the woods and meadows? All would be provided, said the Sermon on the Mount, if we just lived with the faith of the lilies in the field. No footnotes to that teaching. No qualifiers or addenda. All was already there for our well-being and sustenance. We just needed to be alive and decon-ditioned enough to try something new, and with blueberries that meant seizing summer moments to "pick em' and eat em' my whole life through."

# WATER

A cold September portended the winter to come, a premature reminder. I'd become quite adept at handling the physical aspects of country living, but, with summer delights over, my resolve to stay at this cabin began to sag. August crackled dry, and the stream where I got my water trickled to almost nothing. Every two weeks or so I'd make the quarter-mile trek to fill a six-gallon container. The stream originated from an underground spring, so I (perhaps foolishly) never filtered or boiled that water. I never got sick, but I wondered if my healthy luck would eventually run out.

In mid-month I had a disturbing dream that made me think even more about leaving: I'm in the cabin and a flood occurs, sweeping it off its foundation. I'm swirling but unafraid. The water is rising, almost reaching the ceiling. I black out, then awaken (still in the dream) and find the cabin several hundred yards away. My father is there, offering to help get it back with a bulldozer. The dream ends.

*Early fall proved hard. My money, like my water supply, ebbed. Again, as in July, I wondered about the merit of this way of living. But if I left, what would I return to? The city? The small towns nearby? Everything palled after this experience of living alone in a deep-woods cabin. I considered resurrecting my master's degree and becoming a therapist again. Thinking about it, I found that my head throbbed with anxiety. I performed well as a therapist, but it took so much out of me.*

*With all these doubts, basic needs continued needing attention and action. Thirst and a low water jug motivated the movement needed to fetch water from the stream. And once accomplished, the achievement, the water in my jug in my cabin, in some small but powerful way brought a renewed meaning to living in that country place.*

W ithout indoor plumbing connected to the town tap, I had never been farther from my water, yet never closer. Water took on new meaning and perspective when gathered from a small waterfall in the cool density of a northern wood. Water signaled a struggling with, a fighting for, a heaving home. In the spring and early summer, vicious battles with mosquitoes ensued—mosquitoes who must have seen me invading their territory as the Romans saw Attila the Hun. I slipped on mossy rocks, traversed branches, and sometimes suffered a soaking foot or two.

In these conditions water seemed more than mere water: it moved, it lived, like life itself. I set up systems to collect rain, with buckets and barrels set under my most reliable drippings and run-offs. A drought in August made me worry about water—about my garden, about the streams that were rapidly drying up.

Up the mountain was a well that I could tap into, but the water from that well lay lifeless—still and warm. The water from the

*STEPHEN ALTSCHULER*

stream, though, didn't have a chance to warm up. Always moving, it sought out new cool eddies and overhanging lips of moss. And the rocks that I stood on were cold, and the water hugged those rocks, and it leaped them.

One of the first things people I met asked me about was running water. I usually answered in a cute way like "Yeah, I've got running water—runs all the time about a thousand feet away." But I started repeating that to the same people, so I began answering straightforwardly. Other than a phone, it seemed that water was what most people were most unwilling to give up, particularly hot running water for showers and dishwashing and such. I usually presented myself as living proof, however, that a person could get by without it, because I ate pretty well off clean dishes and kept myself clean, since I worked out a system to heat up water by putting a piece of glass over a tub and leaving it out in the sun all day.

I wouldn't recommend it for everyone all the time, but if you tried it on a camping trip, for example—I mean, gathering your water from a nearby mountain stream (by all means, filter or chemically treat it, though, to deal with everpresent contaminants that are common in even the highest mountain sources)—you'll have a better feeling for the water that comes out of your faucet when you return home. It might even taste a little better or look a little more alive, because it once *surged* alive. Rambling down a mountain stream, rippling over rocks and moss and fallen branches, water reigns as one of the great forces of life in our universe.


I read newspaper accounts of water dammed and diverted and polluted, and they always came across as if water was a possession, that we owned it and could manipulate it the way we could a piece of clay. We granted water rights, we tested it, we purified it, we drained it, and we dredged it. We deluded ourselves into believing that we spawned *it* and not that *it* spawned us, for we would all be dead without it. Not just our lawns or our gardens or our automobile engines, but every living thing on this earth would die without water.

A guardian of water should be appointed in each town. I'm not talking about a water department in charge of passively collecting, cleaning, and dispensing it, I'm talking about a person or team of people responsible for following the flow of water in a town and seeking out and eradicating any pollution sources. We already have that, you say: we have planning boards and environmental protection boards and boards of health. Then why can't most people go to a nearby stream or river, as I can, dip a cup in, and drink without collapsing on the spot?

Is there really any other resource or utility or commodity, besides people, that is as important as water? And since the well-being of people is so integrally linked to the well-being of water, can we afford not to guard it more carefully?

The stream was thin after the drought, and I needed to bring a cup and dip it into a shallow pool beneath the tiniest of waterfalls. It took a long time to fill my large container, but the mosquitoes were gone in September, and the woods were beginning to yellow again as the nights turned colder. The cup-by-cup pace renewed my sense of perspective about the reason I came here and the reason I needed to stay longer. It helped me remember my inherent connection with nature, and it got at the essence of my humanness: that living took time and care and attention. And eventually, through perseverance and resolve, the container filled.

*STEPHEN ALTSCHULER*

# THE COLD

In late summer and fall, as money woes continued, I resurrected an old skill and began teaching golf to juniors and guests at a year-round resort inn. Three days a week I walked the fourteen miles round-trip. One day, after the lessons, I rounded a corner to the office, holding clubs in one hand and golf balls in the other, and came face to face with a neighbor's Great Dane, who was relaxing quietly by the door. Up he jumped at my six-foot, one-inch frame and, without having to reach up much, bit me on the hip as I turned away.

I still like dogs, although their unpredictability regarding biting still rattles me some, but after a doctor plunged a million units of somethi-cillin into me, destroying all good and bad bacteria, I contracted four back-to-back colds that gripped me almost the entire winter. This possible sign from universal forces had me wondering seriously about departing this environment that seemed more fit for bears than humans bundled in goose feathers and cotton.

*With misery as a contrary companion, I skied from the cabin to the inn to my job, which now changed to running a ski shop and giving cross-country skiing lessons.*

*The intense cold outside and my state of low immunity made me want to stay no longer in this cabin in the north country woodlands. For the moment, though, given the cold and my lack of a car, I saw no reasonable way out of—or into—an outer reality that set my inner emotional environment to vibrating toward the point of chaos.*

The cold stalked me like a shadow, hovering, enveloping, constantly testing my defenses. It knew every crack and crevice, every structural deficiency, and every exit, entrance, and uncaulked window. It sat out there like an Apache, studying my ways, learning my weaknesses, observing my skills, looking not with eyes but with essence, beyond the ramshackle exterior of this cabin, inward—inward to my soul. For the cold challenged my being, pushed me to know it thoroughly, pushed me to the limits of endurance, and in the pushing, forced me to know and confront those limits.

At the limits of most things lay excitement, uncertainty, anticipation, and fear. And the cold plucked the strings of each, creating an urgent, eerily harmonic arpeggio. Yet the cold, along with its crony, the wind, ultimately warmed me. For just as sour let me know sweet, the cold let me know warmth, let me feel and bask in the radiance of my woodstove, fully stoked and pulsing with hot coals.

Did people who live near the equator know warmth as those who lived farther north did? I doubted it. Our knowing warmth was heightened by our knowing cold. And the cold taught us over and over the ways of warmth, not by showing or telling but, like a good

*STEPHEN ALTSCHULER*

teacher, being a sounding board or mirror reflecting the outcome of our well-laid winter preparations.

One night during a storm the cold found a gaping crevice and invaded my warm oasis in the woods. With gangland brashness it bullied its way past an ill-fitted window that had been one of those repair projects that languished much too far down my "To Do" list. As the wild night progressed, staying warm was my main activity. But the blustery cold waited for my retreat to the sleeping loft—waited until the warmth of wood heat mesmerized and lulled me to sleep—waited like Delilah, in the shadow of night, to cut the tenuous strands that kept me strong and secure—this death cold.

Yes, death cold: a woman in nearby Jaffrey died in December from exposure. The cold killed her. But it was life cold as well, for after it shouldered my window loose and dumped a couple of inches of snow on the floor below it, I awoke and never before sprang to life so quickly from a deep sleep. No self-indulgent lazing about that early morning. No burrowing back beneath the blankets to avoid the reality of the chill morning air and steal a few more warm cat naps.

For as the spray of snow and draft stung my neck, it finally registered that my snug cocoon had more than a minor crack in its perimeter. Up I jumped, fading flashlight in one hand, heavy boot hammer in the other, trying to batten down this rampaging portal. My hands numbed as I hammered and caulked and cursed, all the time shooing away my kittens, who pranced about excitedly as if thinking their keeper was playing with the chaotic window like a ball of string.

I finally nailed the window in place and sat on my bed like a victorious gladiator, knowing I would have to face this cold in battle again. But as my cats rubbed against me for warmth and security, I saw that the cold was not an enemy but one of many messengers to pound on the door of my capacity to endure. And the way I answered the pounding was more important than any result in the ensuing battle. For the path of endurance is a path of self-knowledge, and a path of self-knowledge is the only path toward becoming a full, actualized human being, capable of compassion, the ability to love, and the ability to be loved.

Anything that pushes on the limits of endurance forces a deeper looking at oneself—which is probably why most avoid such tests at all costs. The average home, and the minds behind the curtains, are bastions, with sentries posted at every entry point to guard against the possible intrusion of the forces of discomfort. As a consequence, such homes and the people within are separated from other homes and families in the area, and it is not until disaster hits—flood, fire, earthquake, tornado, hurricane—that the staunch and seemingly impenetrable lines of defense are breached, and people find themselves and their neighbors.

The cold did not bring people together as a flood would, but it did get folks talking to themselves and each other. It bothered us enough to tweak us off our comfort zones and make us look at our own attitudes towards life. How did I handle stress? What if I were to die today or next week or six months from now? . . . would I be living the way I was living that day? Was I stagnating or moving forward on emotional, physical, mental, and spiritual levels? Was I responding ably to this challenge of being a full human being?

If not for the cold and the other wild, primitive forces, I might not have asked such questions and so might have stayed on the surface of life—which felt great when the waters were calm but overwhelming and out of control when the seas got rough. And they *will* get rough, because everyone will go through disease, old age, and death of themselves and loved ones.

The cold, then, was like the strict teacher we all had and hated but ultimately respected and valued. Sometimes we even felt love for such teachers because they demanded so much of us that they prodded us into performing and realizing our potential. When we entered the classroom then we felt less afraid and more prepared inside to recite the day's lessons. We became our own teachers,

*STEPHEN ALTSCHULER*

encouraging ourselves to move higher on the steps of intelligence, creativity, and humanness.

So each time I felt warmth I could remember the cold and thank it for its teachings instead of cringing from its sting. And when I entered the market and said, "It sure is cold out there!" I could remember the fellowship that the cold spawned as my friends and neighbors and I huddled together and supported each other in the struggles of living.

# 24 HEALTH

Eventually, a homeopathic M.D. helped me kick the lingering head cold, and the tilt of the earth's axis toward the sun helped all of us north-woods people kick the outside cold. My mood eased, and I settled into another warm season. But I knew, too, that I would not spend another winter here. My body had taken a beating, and my mind was tired of struggling with its only reference point: itself, myself.

Still, the warmer weather bid me stay longer, and I did. The new-found sun and warmth bolstered my heart and spirit. Early in May, and through the rest of that summer, I resumed teaching golf at the inn, and the contact with people provided me just what I needed after the long, dark, isolating winter. A journal excerpt in July revealed my re-vived attitude toward life: "It strikes me there is some beauty in every-one. It may be a function of my expanding insides, but everyone I've seen today looks good. There have been times in the past when the re-

verse has been true. But today, as the temperature nears eighty, everything looks really fine."

Good health enabled me to come to this cabin. Life in the woods was rigorous enough without having a physical problem to contend with. Until the dog-bite debacle of the previous winter, and since the homeopathic doctor finally cured the series of colds, I maintained that good health. Natural whole foods, good mountain water, a lot of hammer-swinging and saw-pushing, and a minimum of stress all kept me healthy while others were falling like ferns after frost.

The germ that made the rounds during the change in seasons must have taken a look at my place and decided it would rather settle into wall-to-wall, color TV, electric environs instead. If I had realized that, I would have sealed myself in this cabin and surround-ing forest cocoon until the early adolescent fall decided what it would be when it grew up. Stretches of days when it was sixty degrees and sunny one day, forty and raining the next, and sixty-five and raining the next were mighty big guns attacking my and everyone's resistance.

But I masochistically descended into that nether city world of oiled, overheated homes, offices, and shops. I could feel the germ phalanxes advancing every time I stepped into one of those hot boxes. I'd counter with every ounce of backwoods, celestial, cosmic, New Age energy I could muster. Drank natural, unpreserved fruit juice, sipped chamomile tea until nearly addicted, ate gobs of brown rice, whole wheat bread, oatmeal, yogurt, and fresh, made-from-scratch soup. Meditated faithfully every day, sometimes twice, said mantras and sutras, recited quotes from enlightened beings, until the ultimate showdown—Armageddon, the final battle between good and evil. If the fight had been at the cabin, the germs would not have survived. I'd have knocked them out in five.

But, alas, the battlefield lay in Boston in a windowless room at a friend's house, one that, had it been equipped with a hose and running water, would have made an excellent sauna. The germs won. In a final surge they broke through my defenses, and all I could do was hobble back to the cabin, trailing orange peels and maple granola crunch, making sure I had a good supply of hand-kerchiefs on hand.

The cold was a mild one, though, and didn't last long, for I took the best medicine I know—a completely balanced medicine that sometimes takes years to show results but was constantly healing and sustaining and nurturing. I took medicine called "the woods"—not three times a day before each meal, but every moment. The woods, whose individual members at times grew sick, but who lived on.

Outside my window, white pines were dying, stricken by a disease that was rampaging throughout the Northeast. But as they died and fell to winter storms, the space created allowed the hard-wood stands to flourish. The cycle continued, and each member lived with a total trust of the whole of nature, a trust that Snidley Whiplash germs and disease would ultimately be foiled, that the woods—that nature—would in the long haul survive and thrive.

"Who will take care of you if you get sick?" my mother asked before I came to this cabin. When I was a boy, I trusted that she would, and she did. But at age thirty-two, my trust fell on my inner self. And as I trusted more of that inner self, I more fully trusted nature and the woods. I more fully saw myself as an individual and integral part of it.

And as the white pines of my life succumbed and fell, I, like the red maple and oak and birch and cherry around my cabin, felt the nurturing and loving sun and spread out my roots to grow.

# NEIGHBORS

Eventually, utility companies stretched power and telephone lines up Timbertop Road, and a developer started building upscale homes in the forest just a half-mile or so from the cabin. Observing this, I decided to leave that fall, retreating first to a transitional cottage without utilities in a somewhat less remote woodland, one closer to my job at the inn.

The thought of leaving troubled me. I felt confused about my purpose. Another crossroad. What do I want? Where do I go? Time for another reassessing. What do I do? I am worn out from thinking.

And yet, what was there to get out of? Where should I go that I wasn't already there? What should I do that I wasn't already doing? What more about myself should I know that I didn't already know on some level of understanding? Why should I leave, I asked myself? Why should I leave?

But leave I did, grieving for the end of a special time in my life,

*grieving as well for the demise of the natural forest into a country ver-*
*sion of suburbia as well. I grieved for my neighbors, older folks who*
*had lived off Timbertop Road for what seemed forever but whose quiet*
*lives would be irrevocably changed by luxury cars kicking up dust on*
*hot summer days and snowplows plugging up their driveways so com-*
*muters from the development could get their kids to day care or private*
*school on time.*

*Time itself was to change and speed up along the road and into*
*the forest, but the memory of my neighbors would remain the same as I*
*thought of their good hearts and simple generosity.*

Since moving to the New Hampshire countryside I experienced not only the nurturance of the natural environment but the
helpfulness and support of my neighbors. Beneath the crust of Yankee cautiousness, they displayed, for the most part, generosity and
acceptance. I say, "for the most part," for exceptions persisted, like
the young couple who lived in the cabin over the hill who left their
dog alone and tied up and underfed for long hours and days, causing
him to constantly howl and finally break free, running up and down
the road dragging his chain behind. Their cabin burned to the
ground last fall, the result of a cheap tin-plated wood stove, fully
stoked and unattended, and a lot of bad karma.

And my profiteer neighbors pushed their way around as well,
prostituting the forest with telephone and electric lines, and bull-
dozers and chain saws that pushed and cut and slashed the woodland
floor to open a view of Mount Monadnock for houses more suited
to a city than to a forest.

But at the other end of my neighbor spectrum lived people
whose actions reflected their good will. Louie and Agnes, neighbors
of mine about a mile and a half away, extended to me the hospitality

*STEPHEN ALTSCHULER*

of their home, shared their garden produce with their woodchuck-devastated backwoods neighbor, and let me use their phone for emergencies when I occasionally appeared out of the cold night on visits that sometimes led to an unexpected meal and good conversation about the goings-on around town and beyond. Nothing appeared put-on about these people, no pretenses; they were just hardworking and honest and very resourceful—qualities that made a bond between us, even though their dwelling and life situations were much different from mine.

Old Tom lived in the house next to the road: a cautious man. He never invited me inside his place, but I came across no more generous a person since moving to the country. He gave me barrels for my root cellar and rain water system, cans for kerosene, a fine snow tire when I still had the car—he owned a Rumbler, too—help with my car, and—most valuable—lore of the woods, like the best water and wood sources. A Finn, one of many in that region, he quietly displayed a combination of good humor, basic intelligence, economy, and generosity. He used wood heat and had no phone. And although he lived only fifty feet from the highway, he dwelled close to the natural environment and even in his old age maintained a high degree of self-sufficiency. I admired and respected Tom for that.

Other helpful people inhabited the community: the car mechanic in Greenville who spent a half-hour of his own time advising me on the intricacies of my car and who said, after I thanked him, "Hey, we're all in this together. We gotta help each other out." And the poet from Harrisville who gave me a lift in the spring and wound up turning off his car and spending the next hour talking about all sorts of common interests. And, of course, my close-friend neighbors: Al, whose knowledge and feel for the woods I respected greatly; and Ferris, another ex-urbanite—a fellow trier, a doer, a risk-taker in this country adventure . . . and sometimes misadventure.

I may have lived in the woods alone for long hours, but I had a structure of support around me. And as the natural environment ripened with neighbors, each separate, yet intertwined in a web of life silk, so too did people make up each strand in the fabric. And the strength of that fabric grew tight and tested with the care and concern and love each person extended to fellow sojourners in this vast, mysterious universe.

So good fences did not make good neighbors in the country: good will did; and good will abounded all around.

# TWO

# LIVING
# IN THE
# CITY

After almost four years of country and woods living it was time for me to move on. In the New Hampshire wilds I enjoyed a sense of autonomy I hadn't felt anywhere else. And, when I wasn't stirring up the pot with worry, the quiet relaxed me. But I missed something, something I thought at times I didn't need but ultimately did: people and the social and political systems around them.

No matter how much they disappointed me at times, people put me in touch with a part of my humanity that the woods could not. I could be one with the maple tree outside my sleeping loft, I could walk in the woods, clearing my mind and opening my heart, but that sustained and nurtured me just so much. I needed and wanted more social juice, despite its occasional bitterness. I wanted more contact with a part of the world the woods shut out.

So I left, now looking elsewhere for the Holy Grail, traveling for about a year in the United States and Europe, a writer without a home or even a desk, staying for the longest time (a few months) in one place at Cambridge, Massachusetts, to write an eco-tragi-comedy musical (which is still aging in my desk drawer ten years later), then driving to California to . . . well I'm not exactly sure why I came to California. I'd met a woman in Cambridge who had traveled there and, although I expressed doubt and hesitancy, she beckoned me to join her. And I'd heard about the legendary warmth and sunshine, which would allow me to easily hike and walk in natural places year-round. And friends had mentioned the creative atmosphere and commitment to personal growth. And I'd never been. Also, there were tales of the progressive, Zen-sitting governor (Jerry Brown), who appointed a Pulitzer Prize-winning Zen Buddhist poet (Gary Snyder) to head the state's commission on the arts. California twinkled like a unique star, and, after my time in the deep country, offered contact with a wide variety of people and opportunities to spread my own creative wings.

I didn't really intend to stay (does anyone?). In fact, I didn't intend or plan anything at that time, since I fed off the stored energy of several very powerful meditation retreats with a great California-based Japanese Zen Master, Sasaki Roshi. He taught me—without teaching, in a Western sense—to follow my heart and to make decisions accordingly—to feel my own center of gravity and find the thread that connected me to all life. Given the natural beauty of the Bay Area, and that nothing else was attracting me at that time, and that I would have been just as broke anywhere else, I cleared my mind, sensed my center of gravity, and decided to stay. Once again I became a city man, and, being emotionally opened and readied by the Zen training and probably the years at the cabin, quickly met and, a year later, married, a city woman—also a Buddhist meditator, although not practicing the Zen form I was more drawn to.

So I moved into my fiancée's collective house in Berkeley, began writing, working as a therapist, offering meditation workshops for people with eating disorders, and settling into a fairly slow pace for city living. For a short time life seemed idyllic—happy relationship, good home, creative work, spiritual and emotional growth, physical fitness—but cracks began to develop in the levee, caused, in retrospect, and appropriately so for California, by earthquake movements of the soul.

A couple of months after we met and before we married, my fiancée and I attended a three-month Buddhist meditation retreat on the East Coast. Known as Vipassana, this form featured long periods of silent, still meditation, separate quarters for men and women, and even a lack of eye contact between the participants—practices more suited to monks and nuns than to the newly-engaged. (The form derived from the ancient Theravadin school, quite different from Zen in means but similar in its intended end: to awaken and become enlightened.) She and I did not draw closer or understand each other better—neither of which were goals of the retreat. And in the next three years she attended, on her own, three more long-term retreats, while I began retreating not only from this particular form of meditation but from the relationship itself. I understood her spiritual aspirations, but for me, absence made the heart grow distant.

In Berkeley we lived in a very conventional house—albeit a loose collective with three other people—in a conventional residential neighborhood, complete with a gentrified shopping district with store names like Sweet Dreams and Lobelia, selling items totally unnecessary for sustaining, or even enjoying, life at its core. This life was the polar opposite of my previous life in the country, and the effect was unnerving and unsettling.

The marriage and its decline also affected my relationship to the city, steering me to seek places of comfort, which for me meant quiet corners of nature within the city limits and, when I could get away, beyond. So I would take long walks in an attempt to find my niche—just the right remedy for helping to balance my internal life—knowing that walking provided a link to the earth and in doing so became my principal means of meditation.

As I walked the city I became more aware of people, whom I began to see as part of an urban natural environment, part of my expanding view of nature. For despite all the bad press cities got, they did have a diversity of people, who also often got bad press but for the most part weren't as bad as depicted. (Often, they were better than the bad press that gave them bad press!) In fact, people, rather than being separate from the environment, added a whole new dimension to it.

People constituted part of the whole of the environment and were never completely apart from it. The Venerable Thich Naht Hanh, the Vietnamese Zen teacher, writer, and activist, called this situation "interbeing," showing how seemingly isolated things, events, and beings—such as a cloud, food on our plate, and our great-grandfathers—were connected, and, in basic ways, dependent on each other. With that perspective, every one of our acts related to every other action and event in the world.

He portrayed an expansive view that allowed me to include people in what was called the environment, seeing them, yes, as part of the problem, but also as part of the solution and part of what remained right with that environment. We and our cities existed as part of the natural world, and although we might eventually follow the same fate as the dinosaurs, we were probably here to stay for awhile and could make choices that could help and protect rather than destroy and degrade. If the guy in the upstairs apartment in a building where I used to live could have seen his connection with the "natural" neighborhood environment, would he have polluted that environment by playing his drums at 2:00 o'clock in the morning, as he sometimes did?

We might be able to pressure others to be environmentally sensitive through moral, ethical, and legal measures, but essentially, we must feel that "interbeing" with what is around us—including people, places, things, and events—and understand our individual roles in creating excess in order for pollution, in all its manifestations, to stop.

So rather than being angry at the young man upstairs or my other fellow city dwellers who consumed and threw away too much,

I chose to explore my relationship to them and the wildlife (including pets) that lived so close by. It did no good to wish wasteful people away, so, like the eminent city planner/philosopher J. B. Jackson, who founded *Landscape Magazine*, I preferred to look at cities and their inhabitants with an objective eye, to see how they evolved and how people changed toward their home turf and each other. This view connected me more with the homeless, with the perpetrators and victims of crime, with the immigrants struggling with a new language and culture—and the prejudice against them—with stray pets cast away, with orphaned wildlife, with abused children and battered women, with the disabled, with the disenfranchised. It connected me and stirred a greater sense of responsibility that led to taking more action, both with my own life and on a societal level, to make things right.

I watched my own feelings and spirit as well, for they monitored my own understanding of what was around me, perceiving how I both affected and was affected by this urban environment and how I could change myself and the environment. This new view invited a fluid approach that downplayed dogma, opinions, and judgments, emphasizing observation, sensitivity, understanding, and handling with care. It emphasized the Golden Rule.

I came back to the city sensitized by the country. By attending to the details, I found that in their naked essence the two places were the same. People in my city experiences, rather than predominating, represented one aspect of life, blending with birds, creeks, trees, and the changes of the season.

Besides people merging with nature, another merging of supposed opposites seemed to take place simultaneously: a merging of concepts of country and city. They have traditionally indicated separate places, one serene and fresh-aired, the other noisy and dirty. One fresh, young, alive, safe, and innocent; the other jaded, harsh, unfair, deadening, and dangerous. But I began to discover that city contained pockets of elements that would normally be described as country. As I continued my habit of walking about, developed in the New Hampshire woods, I would set out to explore the surrounding ecosystem, discovering parks, creeks, and quiet public paths that put me into a peaceful state.

The Bay Area blossomed in the mid-to late nineteenth century when environmentally conscious planners (influenced by John Muir and John Burroughs) developed aesthetic hillside street designs that favored walkers with quiet public lanes and stairways. Landscape designers often preserved natural places within the cities, with trails and parks providing access. These, along with easily reached mountain trails in the Sierras and throughout the coastal ranges, made northern California, and most immediately the urban Bay Area, a paradise for this walker.

I found the country within the city. My senses filled as if I walked down a country lane. Seeing and feeling everything before me, I tried suspending preconceptions that said the country or the city was better than or more nurturing than the other. The natural environment, then, appeared anywhere my eyes, mind, and heart perceived it, and everything I experienced in the city—even the guy behind the deli counter yelling out the next number—had the potential of being part of the natural urban environment.

To see the naturalness and country-ness of the city and to balance its frenetic energy required a periodic gearing down and remembering the senses. It required, from time to time, a stilling of the thinking mind, settling into a silent space, taking a break from commerce and conversation. It required a re-turning toward an inner spirit that noticed not only the flower but the flower within the flower. That inner flower was the sensitive mind that deemed it important enough to stop and smell, and then realize and revel in what it is doing.

# 26

# THE HI-LINE

*When I arrived in the Bay Area and began settling in, I did indeed meet more people, as I had envisioned I would. For a former adolescent recluse and introvert, this development was extraordinary. The world of people had never been a very comfortable one for me, and my time at the cabin did not particularly increase the skills needed for that world. But some change must have occurred during that self-imposed country retreat, some inner change that made me feel more centered and capable of handling the social interactions. And that centeredness and capability made entering the world of people exhilarating and freeing, something that felt wonderful to this basically shy man.*

*One reason the world of people hadn't been comfortable was its premium on verbal cleverness—which was why I became a writer fairly early in my adulthood: I could take my time with thoughts and words, change them, consider them. Writing, like spending time in the woods, fit* my internal pace better. Everything in the "outside" society seemed fast, bordering on reckless.

The Bay Area, except for its freeways, was a less frenetic urban center than most I'd experienced. People seemed more relaxed and less worried, at least in Berkeley. And for a worrier like me, this general attitude helped ease my characteristic catastrophic thinking, which was pumping away, given my low income despite the several things I was doing for money.

Walking and hiking helped, too, and when I engaged in them, which was almost daily, I noticed others of my species who must also have valued this saner pace. I acknowledged them, and exchanged smiles—which in high places was often.

When I moved back to the city I discovered something I hadn't been aware of before, something I began to acknowledge and study every time it happened: a simple though worldly phenomenon that occurred when taking walks in quiet environs. This phenomenon would not make the evening news. Nor would anyone rush home and report about it. But the moment it happened, a universal alignment took form that immediately affected life on earth. In this moment in time and place people passed and said hello.

Children knew the moment well, and (most) dogs knew it, and, in a non-verbal form of it, folks on country backroads who lifted their index fingers from the steering wheels of relatively slow-moving cars or trucks, hi-ing to passing vehicles or pedestrians, knew it. I called it the "Hi-Line," a noble moment when beings bridged the alienating chasms of modern life. In the rural areas it could occur even in town, at the Post Office, for example, when people smiled and looked you in the eye as they held the door open, even if they didn't know you. This simple act of acknowl-

*STEPHEN ALTSCHULER*

edgement, related to the Hi-Line, was more inherent in country people.

In cities, the Hi-Line usually ensued out and away from congestion, away from fast-moving automobiles in particular. It often manifested in high places, but not necessarily: you could experience the Hi-Line at sea level, on hilltops, and within quiet neighborhood parks. It usually happened near nature, and often under some vast quantity of sky, regardless of that sky's condition. You could find the Hi-Line in a drizzle as well as a drought.

Now within the craw of cities there did exist an "eye-line" when passers-by (and sometimes drivers-by) glanced at each other; but to raise the white flag and say "hi" would have aroused distrust to the point of malice. Usually a grunt, with the decibels of a burp, greeted such an open gesture, as the startled grunter grumbled away. But in more remote and tender places the fewer commercial diversions helped to settle and focus the mind on the greater self-awareness that could heighten sensitivity to other beings. So a simple greeting was often received and returned the way long-time neighbors exchanged garden tools.

Yet at urban Hi-Lines, a "hi" was not automatic. Several group configurations played into it. Whereas one-on-one meetings, in which two people passed each other with no one else around, invariably resulted in some form of salutation, when one person met two the chances of a "hi" tapered off. This did not hold true at backcountry Hi-Lines, where any numbers and combinations of people would always exchange greetings. But near cities the two companions were often so deep in conversation, they didn't even look up. Their talk waxed intense, animated, and serious, allowing little space for a glance, much less a "hi." If one of the talkers should look up and note the passerby, he or she might utter something like a "hi," but it was a loath sound much like the aforementioned eye-line grunt.

Now, if the solitary walker met a group of three or more, significant "hi" activity often took place. Such groups tend to talk more superficially, so all it took was one in the group to look up, acknowledge the fellow walker, and say "hi." At this cue, most of the others "hi"-ed, with the exception of a consistent few who made it a point never to "hi," although even these iconoclasts usually couldn't resist at least a smile.

An even more engaging situation arose out of two-on-two configurations, particularly when romantic involvements prevailed within both parties. At times, if everyone spoke solemnly, the couples might pass each other like commuters in a train station. But more often they signaled tacit acknowledgement of relationships in progress—acknowledgement of risk-taking. So conversations stopped for a moment, and everyone greeted everyone else respectfully. Camaraderie, however brief, reigned.

The Hi-Line transcended the distance, aloofness, and anomie of the city, giving entry into other lives. The sound of the human voice, friendly and open, healed and added harmony to this dissonant world. You didn't have to qualify for a "hi" at the Hi-Line. No applications to fill out. Nobody asked what you did or where you lived or who you voted for. Less judging arose.

Maybe more spaciousness set the tone and agenda. We all had more room to breathe. The air tingled with freshness and vitality, and so did the people. In the congested places, the game required avoiding bumping into objects and people—not easy, given the density. We walk or drive around with blinders, training ourselves to attend only to the task in front—sometimes days in front—of us. We don't see each other except to avoid collision (and, given the statistics, don't do well with that, either).

But places less touched by technology and commerce replenished human contact. Clots dissolved in an environment that nurtured friendliness. Good will and trust ruled the ridges.

Of course, anyone anywhere could draw the Hi-Line. All you'd need to do would be to say "hi" to a passerby. It might be risky. There might be rejection or, worse, no response at all—which might make you feel vulnerable and wishing you'd never said "hi." Or the stranger might smile back and reciprocate with a "Hi, how ya doin'?" causing you to enjoy your openness and notice a renewed lightness to your step. Of course, either way, if you were aware of your reaction and feeling, you couldn't lose: you'd know a little more about yourself and the world. You'd know that you had ventured into unsure territory and survived. Our souls like it when we take such risks, however small.

Considering how few people in the world exchange friendly words with us, the Hi-Line is vital: old, familiar souls can meet there, momentarily, and reassure each other of their inherent affability and good nature.

# 27

# SPRING

It was such a glorious spring, that 1982—my equivalent of the Summer of Love in the San Francisco of '69—for I met the woman who was to become my second wife. Once again, in the midst of warm humanity, I glowed with openness, basking in the warm sun after New Hampshire's cold.

I lived on automatic pilot, and as long as I kept my obsessive head in check, everything bloomed like the orange poppies and blue lupines on the surrounding California hillsides. Even writing ceased, including journal entries, for writing felt too far removed from the actual experience of spring.

I found Spring in the Bay Area a gentle affair. Not so much a burst of bud and blossom but a progression. It didn't arise from death and dormancy, as did a New England spring; rather, a well-groomed *bon vivant*, it put on dressier clothes and stepped out more. Cherry and plum blossoms were the first arrivals—in late February, a timing that was disturbing, and bordering on the macabre, for a former winter-hardened New Englander. Delicate and sweet-smelling, the pink and white blossoms embroidered neighborhood streets. They added variety and luster to the many hues of green painted by winter rains. They brightened a cloudy day; and when their brilliance waned, their falling petals speckled and lightened the dark, wet paths.

The cherry blossoms smelled sweet, and the spring air, cool, fresh, and alive. For a moment, no thought intruded. With "nothing" in the way, boundaries disappeared. Peace prevailed.

In the gardens, purple crocuses appeared—quite suddenly—and in the hills, small shoots of green rose among deadened stalks and branches. I sensed a rising feeling, a welling up, an expansiveness that filled up the dead spaces left by winter. If the universe expanded infinitely, as some said, this spring expressed that expansion.

Each year spring appeared, as if for the first time, the first spring. Nature seemed surprised—delighted, in a way—without memory of the way it was or should be. And without this retention of past images, I rendezvoused with unbridled budding and flowering.

Deep inside, flowering happened, too—deep beneath the layers of memory and programmed thought. Deep beneath ideas of life I discovered life itself, unburdened by meanings or messages, dogma or belief, hope or despair. Life defined life—a bud opening ever so gently in spring—gently yet fearlessly, without doubt or hesitation.

To walk in nature as it bloomed in spring nurtured the spirit. The camellia, so full with flowers that it dripped petals. A new iris braving the early spring cold and rain. Daffodils dressed to the hilt like little girls parading about in their mother's party dresses and high heels. And wildflowers reveling like Mardi gras mummers on the hillsides and shorelines.

It takes a certain slowness to see. Scurrying about, thinking of this and that, obscures the view. For only as the mind quiets can its view, both inner and outer, deepen. And only as that view deepens can the spring inside match the spring outside.

# SACRED PATHS

From the start, I was always trying to make sense of moving to northern California in relation to my life. In May I wrote in my journal: "A new life begins. Moment to moment. Take it all in. It's all just a temporary blip. One little blip in time. What will you do with your blip? How will you live your blip? Right now you're dead and alive together, and neither. What can you do? Can you keep dying? Do you know what living is? Is it different from dying? Breathe in: breathe out. Breathe in: breathe out."

So I sought places that helped me remember to continue breathing and be aware of my breathing. Breathing remained the primary thing I, and everyone alive, had in common, but with the stimuli and pace of the city, I so easily forgot to notice this most vital and basic life function. Sitting on a cushion in meditation, which I and my fiancée did daily, calmed the mind but revealed a need. I required direct contact

*with nature and the world outside of myself, a world that reflected my*
*true self when I paid attention to the cadence and spirit of its breath.*

The idea of holding certain paths sacred was not a new one.
Holy ground, power spots, roads to Mecca, sacred pilgrimages:
most of the major religions had them, American Indians have them,
Thoreau had his, Annie Dillard has hers, and John Muir had many.
One of mine was in Oakland, and although it was not as grand as
Tuolumne Meadows trails in Yosemite it provided a similar feeling.
It acted as a screen that filtered out particulate mental matter. And
in the pace of the city, such miasma built up quickly. Sometimes
any walking will clear the channels, will slow the motion picture
frames enough for us to regain perspective, to remember the who,
what, and why of living on this planet.

The answers to these questions were not attainable to me when
driving a car or watching television or talking a blue streak. But
when out walking, or being still and quiet and taking in what was
around, I found that the answers came more easily.

At those times, humanness abounded, humanness characterized by the walking, the quiet, the taking in. Could humanness
really be that simple? For I learned, through socialization, not to
trust simplicity. Advertising didn't promote simplicity. No one considered simplicity sexy, and it didn't cost much, so most devalued
it. Adults offered little support for staying simple when growing up.
They encouraged conspicuous spending and the satisfaction of desires, and they indulged in such behavior themselves. All that took
time, money, and technology. Something like walking didn't add
to the Gross National Product. So I, like practically everyone, be-

*STEPHEN ALTSCHULER*

came drunk . . . with cars and TV and electric can openers and shopping malls.

It took living in a cabin in the woods for several years to break some of the habits and mold new values. But upon returning to the Madison Avenue world, I realized a need for reminders of those values that had been reshaped in the North Woods. It was nature, and places removed somewhat from the world, places not far from home that had the spirit of the woods, that provided a nurturing of some simple spirit deep within.

Some of these trails lay quite close by. But one trail had something even more special: a certain quietude, a certain affinity, a certain feeling that the trail birthed part of my spirit. Difficult even to write about. A feeling beyond words, deep in the heart of the trail, communicated more through the feet. Strange to think of the feet as receptors, but the feet garnered what the trail gave. The mind remained too enamored of the material world to hear the nuances of the trail, the fine-pitched creaks and rumblings of deep earth, the shifts in elevation, the coursing of underground water, the rise and fall of temperature as rotted matter and shadows and sun combined to cause subtle changes.

Long ago we went barefoot, and our feet were more sensitive to the earth. But even through Vibram soles we can hear what the earth—the trail—is saying. On a spirit trail the earth speaks directly, and what is received is often a gift of forces deep within nature.

Intimacy grew with walking the same trail many times, and to be intimate with anything or anyone resulted in a losing of the self in the other and becoming aware of losing that self. Then, if I had a question to present to the spirit trail, less complexity, born from preoccupation with the self, fogged the emergence of the truth. While this might sound a bit cryptic and mystical—and perhaps a spirit trail rendered that in part—the clarity and simplicity of the answers kept them from being cryptic.

Yet the value and essence of a spirit trail extended beyond the answers to questions. The essence drew breath from the communing itself. The essence lived in the feet's contact with the earth. A re-connection. A re-turning of an evolutionary wheel that once knew walking as a miraculous act, much as parents know it today when their child takes that first step. Any trail, any path, then, could be a spirit trail at any moment. It needed only my remembering the marvel of walking on this earth.

# WALKING TOGETHER

     The most glaring difference between life in the city and life in the country surfaced as people, measured in quantity and quality of contact. The city had more, but most of them had less time to spend in such non-productive pursuits as walking. Since the sixties, people in Berkeley remained more "laid back" than those in most of North America, but the endangered species list included anyone out walking leisurely in mid-week. People worked, produced, created, made love—I don't know, they stayed somewhere inside, out of sight.

     So feelings of isolation in the city environment sometimes developed. In some ways, if I wanted to be with people and could find no one to walk with, that feeling grew more intense in the city than in the country, where I hadn't expected to connect with anyone. The city bur-

*geoned with people, but most appeared too busy—even too busy relaxing—to take a walk break.*

*My fianceé (along with a few close friends) represented an exception, since she had figured out how to make a rather nice living working only two days a week. And I had resorted to living off credit cards—I called it "living with interest"—trying to sell freelance articles and essays, playing music in nursing homes, and practicing psychotherapy illegally (I had a master's degree in counseling but no state-approved license). I felt as carefree as a Congressman adding to the pork-barrel deficit, so I would seek out people to walk with and explore what looked like an urban Shangri-La.*

*With Thoreau as a model, I sauntered a lot that summer, sometimes alone, sometimes with people, and always "with interest."*

Occasionally, I walked city paths or hilly trails with friends, or with a visiting out-of-town relative when I offered a taste of the city behind the city. I noticed an entirely different quality in walking together compared with walking alone. Many details around, above, and below got lost in the social contacting. But that social contact became richer in the context of that detailed background. Specific flowers might go unseen, but human beings walking together, relating, laughing, sharing, could add to the environment—really, were part of the environment.

Such walking challenged "harmonic convergence," though. We all had different paces, a different inner sense of time, different desire systems and needs. Walking together created an orchestra of separate musicians, and the skill of the symphony depended on the ability of each member to maintain individual talents while sacrificing individuality for the common good. And like an orchestra, walking together presented a good lesson in cooperation: to be

*STEPHEN ALTSCHULER*

effective (and with walking, that meant fun), then adjustments must be made, deals struck, and compromises entered into.

Sometimes walking together might mean letting go completely of your pace in deference to the other person. When strolling with Jean, a good friend born in 1900, I could go no faster than she, which, for a five-mile-an-hour speedster, required quite a letting-go. Our occasional walks beside Strawberry Creek, though, radiated with harmony and joy as we named the trees, reviewed the garden, and listened to the quiet summer creek.

And when I walked with my five-year-old friend, Ben, our route seemed never to follow the straight line I was so accustomed to when walking alone. We veered this way for a mud puddle (to walk in it, not around it!), that way for a butterfly, and yet another way to see a water strider in a creek. Ben personified the essense of sauntering, a movement antithetical to speeding along in a one-pointed direction. His little legs and curious mind would not have allowed that.

To be in a situation requiring adaptation challenged the status quo of the mind—ultimately, a good situation in which my ego didn't get to do everything exactly as it wanted. Walking together, for example, could sometimes stretch that spoiled brat of an ego to its limit.

One day in June I went with two friends up to Tilden Park, a wonderful expanse of open space above Berkeley, for a hike along the Skyline Trail. We must have looked funny—the three of us strung out at one point with the fastest strider, Bob, in the lead, me in the middle, and Morgen last in line on this wide trail. This stringing-out went on for awhile, but somehow, without saying anything, we eventually drew even with each other and stayed that way for the rest of the hike, with Bob champing at the bit at times a few steps ahead. You could just see the ebbing and flowing of alone/together energy as each tried to silently compensate for the other's presence and pace. We performed a sort of dance, choreographed by the forces of nature that required a tithing toward the commonwealth. We enjoyed each other's company, not because of willful egos vying for center stage but because of the consideration we each had for one another. If we hadn't been sensitive we might have just as well walked alone and given up the charade.

I still walked alone more than with others during those early re-entry days in the city. I valued such walking, and it nurtured me. But walking together forced a constantly changing examination of the inner self in relation to the outer environment. I couldn't be the free-flying hawk, the lone wolf, the rugged individualist to the same degree as in my cabin days. My awareness of a connection to everything else heightened. My small mind, putting me at the center of the universe and exposed for what it was, betrayed itself as an illusion . . . a delusion, really. In walking with others, I recognized that small minds often faded away, revealing one pace, one pulse, one ultimately peaceful unit not separate from the earth that brought the whole symphony together.

# TOWN CATS

Although as a boy I hated cats indiscriminately, my New Hampshire experience endeared me to these pets. And the woman I'd become engaged to typified those zealous cat people (and an animal rights activist) who rescued strays and adopted them out, not just to the first taker but to people she would screen carefully to determine how capable they would be as "parents." I got inspired by her enthusiasm and compassion, so when the opportunity arose to be foster parents for an orphaned litter (through a program started by the renowned San Francisco S.P.C.A), we seized the day.

In the country the fate of cats hinged, more or less, on the economy of their owners. People displayed a laissez faire attitude, trusting that they—the cats, that is—would, when pressed, find a way to get by, even in the face of dire disregard. But city cats were far more dependent upon people and identified with them more; hence foster parent programs to minister to the abandoned. Country cats, like country people, often knew how to survive on their own. City strays, like city people, often relied on some outside agency to cope with the rigors of society's benign neglect (even in Berkeley, which, for those unfamiliar with it, had been, since the Free Speech Movement there in the 1960s, one of America's most politically and socially progressive, and at times radical, cities—although a Yuppie epidemic in the 1980s drove it considerably to the right).

So we became surrogate parents, bottle feeding and wiping tushies, and finally adopting out all of the litter except one, which we kept. We also marched in animal rights demonstrations, protesting the use and abuse of animals in research laboratories at the University of California at Davis and Berkeley as well as at Stanford University.

But when I wasn't marching, or trying to generate more freelance work, or helping my fiancée take a stray to the San Francisco S.P.C.A., or wiping behinds, I walked the neighborhoods, recording silent notes on the functions and dysfunctions of city cats and those who kept them—including me and our little long-haired orphan named Lila (meaning "the dance of life" in Sanskrit)—a confirmed kitten and near-child whom I loved more than any being I'd ever loved.


As I discovered in the Bay Area (as well as in Boston, parts of New Hampshire, Providence, Philadelphia, and a few other cities I'd lived in), to know a town meant needing to know its cats. In fact, to know any populace (the world over, I'd guess), you just needed to observe their cats, or that they had no cats, or that they took their cats for Sunday drives in the family Volvo station wagon or ox cart. Some city people, of course, owned dogs instead of cats, but with dogs you could tell more about the physiognomy of their owners rather than their psychology. I once knew an elderly man who yapped and waddled right along with his little mutzies.

Cats unraveled the tucked-away threads of people's lives and so the true fabric of a community. Some moved in cautious ways. Other bold, brassy types pranced up as I walked by, rubbed up against my leg, and practically invited me in for tea. Then there were those who hid out behind the house, even behind the garage, peeking out, dreading the possibility of approaching footsteps. Their owners, too, skulked behind the living room curtains peering out through the slit, hardly breathing, waiting, worrying, wishing the interlopers away. Or those slinky longhairs who sidled up and turned so easily, so willingly, on their backs, seducing each passerby who took the time to stop, reach down, and give a kitzle behind the ears. Their owners could often be found puttering around the front yard, greeting everyone in sight.

Then, of course, I noted the daredevils, those stunt cats who darted across the street to attack a tree, leaping ten feet in one lunge, then falling and following a passerby for a block or so, creating the inherited-stray illusion, one of the oldest cat-versus-person tricks in the book. Outside these houses, look for the red Mustang convertible with a Grateful Dead sticker on the rear window. The owners of these cats could often be found at Chinese restaurants ordering dishes marked "hot and spicy" or could be seen at sidewalk cafés with large tropical birds on their shoulders.

Finally, my observations led to that cat—usually a domestic shorthair—who sat most of the day on an elevated spot near the sidewalk in warm weather and inside the front window in cold, watching the passing scene: alert, aware, sensitive, a correct cat in every way, not too timid, not too forward, not too needy, not too aloof—a cat who would rather be alone or with its own kind than ingratiate itself at the foot of some human. A savvy cat who knew something of life, who'd been around, as they say, who'd tasted the milk and the meat, the boudoir and the street, who didn't respond right away when called, lifting an eyelid to see if the call was worth heeding, a cat who saw the mouse but merely recorded a memo in its mental notebook for future reference, who took nothing at face value but who considered and weighed the implications, a cat who mulled it over before acting. A cat's cat.

Cats like that proved tough to find. They chose private spots where they groomed themselves often but didn't make a show of it. They seemed to love routine, sitting day in and day out in the same places. But this charade set up the no-change game that made people think of them as boring and just not worth the time to seek out. The owners of these cats rarely had their houses robbed and seemed chronically unemployed but always had enough money. They had divorced long ago, and they remained happy. They ordered out for pizza a lot, had their morning coffee at popular cafés, and wrote off every waking minute on their tax returns, never seeming to get audited.

So, you see, I began to know towns and cities by observing their cats very closely. Unlike dogs, who came slobbering up totally open and direct, cats had their enigmatic ways. They defied being pinned down from day to day. Nobody could predict the direction a cat would go, or when it would go, or who it would go with. But cats themselves knew the score exactly and, as a result, had their resident towns sewed up. They even had their own master plan, and everything proceeded right on schedule. In fact, it might not be true for your town, but I would say that Berkeley is what it is today because of its cats. That's a bold statement, I know. But facts are facts. And cats are cats.

Oh, my notes reveal one other kind of cat. Not a pedigreed cat, but a rare breed that had never lost its kitten-ish ways: the eternal play-er, that more-than-forty-months old whom the cat food manufacturers referred to as "a mature adult" but who still chased its tail, got excited by water flushing down the toilet, and licked necks as if still nursing. This cat, despite advancing years, would jump six feet straight up to swat a dangling wire, go ga-ga over birds and butterflies, and love to "help" make the bed by diving under the sheets as they wafted down. It cared little for the nuts and bolts of being a cat—the workaday cat world of taking little

*STEPHEN ALTSCHULER*

bites at a time, having short naps, and grooming itself periodically. This cat played like hell, then pooped out for a few hours. The owners of such cats generally enjoyed life. They played a lot, of course, They smiled and laughed a lot, and they rested often. They could, at times, be seen picking plums from neighborhood trees, they almost never washed their cars, and they grabbed a few hours, here and there, to write books like this one.

# RAIN WALKING

      In the fall of 1982 my fiancée and I traveled to central Massachusetts to participate in a three-month silent Buddhist meditation retreat. Now, this may seem like an odd thing for a couple engaged to be married to be doing, but at the time my fiancée was quite interested in this form of spiritual practice, and I was quite interested in her. At this stage in our relationship I wasn't particularly motivated to go sit in silent meditation, but I justified doing it by thinking the experience would bring us even closer together.

      Instead, it stirred a deep cauldron of fear within me, for all this exploration of my mind uncovered some shadowy stuff that went right to the core of my being, without any embroidery or frills to get in the way. I felt a sense of urgency that eventually developed into a full-blown mid-life crisis.

      Coming back to Berkeley, I returned to practical worries of money, job, health, and home, and descended into the ashes from there. I told myself, "Worry not of the morrow. Be like the lilies of the field. Have faith, good man. The way will be shown. Just lean into the unknown. Trust. Flow. Laugh. Dance. Sit." But panic tried to push in. Master of catastrophic thinking, that's me.

I racked my brain for money-making schemes: I could sell my car. I could write books on walking in the Bay Area.* I could get my therapy license and set up a legitimate practice. None of these thoughts consoled me, though.

I reflected a lot—sometimes remembering, sometimes lamenting. But when I thought my life through, I saw that nothing could be changed or returned to, so continuing to wallow in past thought simply wasted time. I saw that the future could never be predicted except that one day I would die like every living thing before me. And I saw ever more graphically that I needed to reaffirm my commitment to trusting the present moment. Within it freedom nestled—freedom from all doubt, fear, worry, and delusion.

The heavy rains of that year somehow comforted me, making me all the more contemplative, keeping me inside more and blurring the view from the windows. Ironically, I was colder here in a California city than I'd been in my cabin, since here it turned out to be so expensive to use the house heat. In New Hampshire I could control the heat according to my willingness to carry in, cut, and split firewood. But in this Golden State house, all of us walked around in down vests, wool caps, and heavy woollen socks. Along with my existential dilemmas, this cold just wasn't the way life was

*Eight years later I did exactly that, publishing *Hidden Walks in the Bay Area* in 1990 and *More Hidden Walks in the Bay Area* in 1991 (Western Tanager Press, Santa Cruz).

*STEPHEN ALTSCHULER*

supposed to be in sunny California. But when did life always roll over when I commanded?

# FIRST RAIN

In coastal California, the first sustained rain (somewhat equivalent in spirit to the first snow in other parts of the country), came after the long dry season that stretched from May through September and sometimes beyond. And in my first year there, the first rain fell like down feathers. It would have been nice to walk nude in it, but alas, the Bay Area, and this walker, had grown more conservative. So a rain parka covered me, although the need for protection seemed a dubious one.

For this rain qualified as barely more than a fog. And yet, in northern coastal California, a fog formed the stuff of summer. A fog moved, roiled unsettled in swirls, rushing toward the hills. A fog shifted asymmetrically. You never knew where it would turn next. You could escape a fog in the hills east of San Francisco Bay—in the regional park, high up on the Skyline Trail, where with a sweep of the head you could on a clear day see five counties and the high Sierras, and probably as many eco-systems and micro-climates (within a radius of ten miles of those hills the temperature could range from fifty to ninety degrees Fahrenheit!). From that aerie the bay and its surrounding cities shivered hidden, filled up with fog to the ridge-tops.

But this rain—this first rain—figured to be more than a fog. Still, settled, secure in its mission, it delivered the message of winter's salvation. The message of rain: a reminder that rain and snow shaped the land of California. Take away rain, and California would be a desert. People knew this and worried perennially about drought.

The weather people and water managers told us it was not enough, this rain. As they shook their doomsayer heads, they told us we were that many inches below normal. Yet this first rain offered hope. Despite all the rain we would need to avoid drought, this first rain heralded a message no more complicated and no less awesome than the simple, familiar sentence we all used so glibly: "It's raining."

When it rained, to protect California newts starting to migrate across the road to their mating and spawning pools, the authorities closed South Park Drive in Tilden Park to cars and bicycles. This rain, then, was very important to newts, helping fulfill something ancient and alive. It, and the compassion and wisdom of human beings, would allow their species to continue, and on some level the newts knew this, I'm sure, feeling the benediction of the rain with every pore and nerve and perhaps noticing the lack of cars that used to crush them and their innocent ancestors.

The rain as benediction. After months of unsettling dryness, it didn't signal that we, too, should head to our mating grounds, but, as it did for the newt, it moistened and settled on our skins. It was a reminder of a watery composition, a time when we all breathed like fish in our mothers' amniotic fluid. So was there really a need to protect against it?

The drought heightened awareness of it, the way absence did of a good old friend. This first rain seemed to caress the earth, and its rivulets ran like tears—tears of deep communion with living things that marveled at it rather than measured it.


## WALKING IN RAIN

Word of rain coming rolled off the tongue so easily, without a trace of awe. People predicted it, bemoaned it, demeaned it, tried to pray it away, as if it were sent just to foil our weekend plans. Then when droughts hit, we beat our chests, vowing never to vilify rain again.

Walking in rain reminded me of strolling with a good friend on a Sunday afternoon. Finding no resistance to its wetness, it came in many forms—a bouquet of mist, a penetrating downpour, a slow, steady drizzle, a wild storm. Each rain arrived with a different expression yet was somehow connected to all the rains that ever fell.

Reflection came easier in rain. The wetness directed thoughts inward. A rainy day afforded a good time to walk alone—slowly, without any direction. A good time for mulling, focusing on a problem rather than on its solution.

Rain bid us all to be still, to slow down: to sip a cup of tea, or hold a lover's hand, or allow one's cat to sit undisturbed on one's lap for a couple of hours. Clarity and peace came. Problems were not so big. Worry didn't last.

The storm had passed, and a patch of pale blue sky appeared. The inwardness rain cultivated helped prepare for the outwardness of the clearing. The sun gleamed in the late afternoon, and damp streets reflected the gilded edges of things. Dark clouds drifted east, still dense and serious. The rain had softened the landscape, had rounded its corners. Millions of clear droplets clung to all they touched. Lines of distinction disappeared, revealing a crystalline embroidery that unified the world. The light over the hills made the mundane magical.

The rain had nourished the earth. Energies rose after the fall. It was a good time to be out walking. Smells from eucalyptus and live oak and redwood freshened and filled the senses while rejuvenating the mind. It was a good time for walking without destination. The street was quieter and the songs of birds clearer. It was a good time for breathing deeply and contemplating ordinary things.

# 32

# WILDNESS

The wild hills east of San Francisco Bay were important places of refuge for me during difficult times emotionally and spiritually. The winters were cool and rainy, but not harsh, like New England's, so I could relax as I hiked and let my mind meander from thought to thought. The hills gave me a breather—literally, a place I could breathe more easily without having to insulate myself as much from the weather, from the nature around me.

The winter sky in the hills changed constantly. Within a day the recipe could include wind, sun, rain, and clouds. I would take my journal on jaunts into the hills and nestle into a world that seemed to give permission to both open up and confront my inner shadows and feel the joy of the moment in a nature wilder than in the city below.

$W$alking in wild places agreed with this urban dweller. The free wind, the swaying grasses and trees, the music of birds, the squish of mud slipped easily from my memory as I rushed about my daily routines. The drone of material accumulation and conspicuous consumption deadened the spirit, so visiting a place where no such activities occurred was rejuvenating.

Fortunately, during the Great Depression wise people had the foresight, sensitivity, and courage to set up, in the hills immediately east of San Francisco Bay, a regional park system that made a portion of this open space wild forever. Otherwise that whole expanse of parkland would eventually have been neighborhoods.

These hills helped quiet my mind. They were innocent and alive, unconcerned with getting something or somewhere, uninterested in gaining position, power, or status, indifferent to image or sex appeal or political persuasion. Beings were born there without great celebration, and beings died there without remorse. Beings received and gave there without judgement. Living things there did not need to work on getting balanced or centered. Their cores were in balance.

The pace of life meandered there, in this place that really had no pace at all—a place that, without the labels of geology, would be of no time, no sense of past, present, or future. To walk in a timeless place must at some level make us whole and resonate with the part of us that is perfectly at ease.

The open hills above Berkeley, at least part of them, suggested such a place. Its magnanimous voice announced with a fresh breeze, "Welcome, walk here in peace." The hills never turned me away. Nor did they beckon. They just existed directly, expecting nothing, giving everything.

I remember a late afternoon in winter when I met mud and

*STEPHEN ALTSCHULER*

fog there, a penetrating fog that obscured all outward views but opened up inner ones. I simply took a walk in the fog in a wild place. Even the self involved in the walking was minimized, for in dense fog, in a place with no houses, cars, or stores, fewer reference points stirred the awareness of "me." In fact, no longer were there any memories of this familiar Big Springs trail, for the fog erased them. The fog made it much less possible to name what was seen, so without the mental activity of naming, a direct relationship followed, a direct connection with the wild hills.

And with that connection the essence of the hills and the walker of the hills were revealed. Something unnameable. Something without time. Something wild, untamed, yet completely disciplined and in order. Being in such communion with the environment renewed and healed me, more healing than any human contrivance or word. For it had little to do with the will. It came uninvited, gently.

These hills did not want or seek. They did not look forward to or look back at. They did not make changes. Changes just happened. They did not wish the bad ones away or hope for the good ones. Only innocence and sensitivity powered their *modus operandi*, and with innocence and sensitivity, ironically, came maturity.

Being mature, the wild hills extended a trusting hand, completely open and vulnerable, receptive to all, resisting none. And without resistance or expectation, in a moment of change and communion the heart opened. No fear. No doubt. No analyzing or processing. No you or I.

Soon after that day in the fog I awoke and saw the hills covered with filtered morning light. The misty hills tendered a spirit that called to all spirits to stop for a moment and look—and in the Bay Area that could be from just about anywhere. To notice them in the middle of a busy day settled the mind in a way no thought or word could.

The hills felt like friends then. Their soft contours conveyed an ease with life, with change. The wildness within the hills endured firmly rooted, forever offering respite and good company.

# 33 BIRDS

In February life began to accelerate as money and career pressures, an impending marriage, and advancing age advanced. At thirty-seven, I began feeling that I'd had my fun (which really didn't seem like much fun at all, when I thought back), and now came the time to roll up my sleeves and bear down on making something of my life (whatever that cliché was supposed to mean). I overcompensated, though. A whirlwind commenced. I applied for nursing-home music grants, held meditation/awareness workshops, worked on a book-length manuscript, renewed my therapy practice, got married, taught at a community college. From the slowest-of-the-slow New Hampshire track to Indy-500 urban life. Fast. Too fast.

I felt vulnerable, as if I wasn't in control of my destiny, and control has always been something I've wanted to be in. Of course, the more I feared being out of control, the more the universe piled on the lessons of control. I tried to hold onto the roller coaster (a couple of *blowout arguments with my fiancée even made me wonder about the planned wedding) by using the crazy wisdom of Zen, giving myself good old-fashioned pep talks, and experiencing nature as ways of balancing the frenetic pace.*

*Birds in the city offered not a remedy but a respite for a mind weary with the worries and struggles of this more complicated urban life. They helped me also remember the mantra, "STAY AWAKE!" which in itself was supposed to act as a reminder of what being a human being was all about, a reminder I sometimes forgot.*

When I walked on a busy street, a street lined with trees, I often stopped for a moment to listen. Up above the noise of traffic and commerce, in the trees, a chorus had often gathered, singing at full volume, a chorus of songbirds—reminders that where all our streets and buildings and wires and poles are, wilderness once was. People could cut down trees to let more light into living rooms, could bury parks under parking lots, and dam, divert, and force streams underground, but less could be done about birds. Despite our assault on wildness, birds continued to live among us (although, according to the scientists, songbirds have been increasingly, and alarmingly, reduced in number).

That birds have survived the past 200 years is extraordinary. Although most other wild species have left our environs or become extinct in the wake of noise, exhaust fumes, industrial and domestic wastes, and commercial construction and housing, birds have stayed close, persevering, adapting to our abuses. And not only have they stayed, they sang and soared quite joyfully, it seemed.

Stopping for a moment, quieting my internal chatter, I could hear sounds that were here long before human technology came and will be here long after technology crumbled. Bird song could

*STEPHEN ALTSCHULER*

penetrate the noise of both motor and mind, but only for a hearer willing to harvest the sounds of the moment.

In and above the city two birds had a particular effect on me. I discerned no sound from these birds, so the impact was more visual than auditory. The hummingbird seemed to have such fun with life. Even its work of food-gathering looked like play. Consider the neon-green Anna's Hummingbird I saw once at a cool waterfall. As it perched on a protruding rock it repeatedly stuck its needle beak into the water, seemingly titillated by the movement of the water, because it often leapt off the rock to dip and sip, flying away, then returning, absorbed in the play of it. Its work and play were the same, fully integrated. How would it be to live with such lightness and joy?

My other favorite, the Red-tailed Hawk, I saw up in the hills gliding and soaring high above the houses and streets. The Red-tail must have been at play, too—a wind bird, so skilled in flight that it wasted not an erg. How would it be to fly with the hawk? To be without the burden of effort, of struggle, allowing the currents of life to set the course? The Red-tail responded almost instantaneously to the changes of wind, not out of habit or knowledge but from its oneness with the wind. It responded to the wind and chose which way to fly—swiftly, effortlessly, simply.

Was it possible to live like the hummingbird and hawk? To come right up to the face of life and sip its water, or soar with changing currents? To see with a fresh eye, hear with an innocent ear, think with an unfettered mind?

As the hummingbird, hawk, and songbird showed, life could be fun—even its daily routines. Daily life meant singing, sipping, soaring without a moment's doubt, with total trust in the truth of the present.

# 34

# FLOWERS

*With my wedding a month away, I put my doubts aside and helped with the necessary decisions. I put other pressing matters like money worries temporarily on hold. And whenever I could, I walked to keep in check my anxiety, which always threatened to burst through my defense mechanisms. Flowers and gardens blooming in March and early April massaged my temples with their gentle fingers. Like birds they also reminded me to STAY AWAKE!—reminders that the Buddha was everywhere: pain, pleasure, anxiety, joy, sadness, anger—all was Buddha.*

Of all the living things I encountered in the city, flowers touched me deepest. They were the universe dancing. But to really see their dance I needed to descend from my observer throne and dance with the observed.

Without my attention to the dance, they remained merely pretty flowers, noted casually in passing, as a bright teapot would be noticed in the hardware store window. If I was talking incessantly or thinking or "exercising," I would miss the dance. I would miss the smell of the jasmine, the grace of the columbine, the innocence of the daisy. I might carry my nature guides and learn the names studiously, but if I missed the flowers dancing, the knowledge I gained from the guides would not have been worth it.

Flowers were the city's most expansive residents. They didn't hold back what they had to give. They didn't *decide* to give out their beauty. They gave it, and they gave it freely, without the slightest hesitation. In living so, flowers epitomized joy.

Walking among flowers I became aware that really communing with them required a certain purity that came with an absence of desire. I simply needed to be present, neither wanting nor rejecting but experiencing. Flowers were sensitive, as scientists reported— sensitive, perhaps, even to a covetous mind that relayed the message to the hand to pick the desired object. Could they know when they were being coveted and sense the moment before they were plucked? Could beings of such beauty, simplicity, and delicacy be affected even by thought?

My relationship with, and understanding of, flowers deepened the year before moving to the city during a Zen *sesshin* with Sasaki Roshi, the Zen Master I mentioned before. In my personal interviews with him (a part of the retreat called *Sanzen*) the Roshi used a flower to get me to drop my thinking mind and realize my true nature, my true self, the part of me that never died. He instructed me skillfully, although with typical Zen ambiguity, to essentially become the flower—not physically become it, but to drop my thinking mind for a moment and see if anything was between the flower and my self that was seeing it. Four interviews a day for seven days we did this, and finally, through practice and great effort, I Saw the flower. I began to cry, sobbing tears that came from some released source inside me, tears of joy and connection with that flower.

Maybe, too, it was the flower's innocence I felt, linked somehow to my own innocence, long since lost. I saw the inner beauty of the flower through the Roshi's guidance, and in experiencing that, I saw a part of my own beauty that I had denied or repressed somewhere along the line. The flower did not contend with me: it just let me in any time I was ready to trust it and myself—any time I was ready to let go of the armor surrounding my true nature.

Walking the streets and reviewing the well-kept gardens, I noticed there were more flowers in the city than the country, cultivated flowers and landscaped gardens (and in Berkeley, flowers of one variety or another were in bloom year-round!), which made me very happy when I saw them. Through my communion with that one flower presented by Buddha-like Sasaki Roshi, I had realized the true nature and beauty of the flower and of myself. And although I lost that realization at times in the din of ego wars, I never forfeited the essence of that teaching.

Flowers enlightened the nature and appearance of the city. They mirrored my own nature as well, reminding me of the legacy of joy that I, and all beings, could receive upon re-awakening to, and dancing with, life.

# THE HI-LINE
# REVISITED

The previous month had been one of the more momentous in my life. In late May my fiancée and I got married, California-style: outside, in a spray of rain, on Mount Tamalpais, the most prominent natural feature in Marin County and the highest point in the immediate Bay Area. We looked like latter-day flower children, with her dress coming from a local flea market and my attire a pull-over, naturally-dyed cotton top and drawstring pants of the same fabric, both bought in Santa Cruz. We held a pot-luck reception, with only one cousin from my family attending, no one from hers, a couple of my long-time New England friends who flew in, and some new friends, mainly from our meditation contacts, filling out the guest list. "Quite a time," I wrote a few days later. "Quite a time. Again, a married man. I never thought it would happen again. And this will be the last and final effort."

*Soon after, as I allowed my spirits to soar into . . . I wasn't quite sure, since I felt a bit wobbly with all the changes, I recorded in my journal: "What wonders await me? Don't know. The content really doesn't matter. It's just a drama. The scenes will change. There's nothing to be done. Just feel your center—feel your center beyond your center. That which doesn't flap in the wind. That which knows all and knows nothing. The center beyond thought of center or wish for center. The center where all the tears and belly laughs dance together."*

*It was an outward time—of being in the world, noticing people, making friends, pursuing work contacts, making application for this or that work. Even hiking became people-centered, since eye contact helped keep me grounded and less in my head. I hiked the hills alone, mostly, since for some reason my wife didn't like these higher, wilder areas, and the Hi-Line served as a friendly way-station.*

Research continued to pour in on further Hi-Line activity—sort of a walking Gallup Poll—and the results pointed to new trends at places out and away from urban congestion. First, some significant racial and ethnic data: very rarely did a person from a racial or ethnic minority venture up to a Hi-Line area. My staff didn't know exactly why this was so, but when it did happen, little "hi" contact transpired. We suspected racism, ethnocentricity, and/or xenophobia, so we've sent this raw data to our Congressperson, urging the creation of a Joint Congressional Commission on Barriers to Saying "Hi" in High Places (JCCOBTSHIHP). To date, the research department has had no response. PR suggested we develop a more euphonious name and abbreviation.

Next, we've also uncovered a stark gender-related truth, reflecting, perhaps, the current state of male/female relations in our culture: when a single man passed a single woman of similar age,

*STEPHEN ALTSCHULER*

they often exchanged no "hi" because the woman steadfastly refused to look at the man, whom she perceived might harm her or ask her for the time as a pretext to asking her to join him for an ice cream cone and then a date and then who-knows-what. If the man said "hi" anyway, the woman would usually utter a reply, sans smile, and never break her stride, which she would quicken and lengthen. Exceptions to this occurred (and probably marriages have resulted from such Hi-Line encounters), but rarely did the two exchange anything more than a "hi," nor did the woman often look back— probably wise of her, given the possibility of horrific road and trailside crimes.

A tendency showed up, too, this time for walkers going in the same direction to ignore each other when one passed the other. This indicated a peculiar one-on-one opposite-gender anomaly here, but it also held for most one-on-two and other multi-walker configurations. In fact, at times the woman would pause and feign an aching back or a stone in her shoe (but never to check a map, since that would invariably draw the man to ask if he could be of assistance), or to pull out a sweater, letting the man go by, thus gaining a degree of control over what she perceived as a potentially dangerous situation.

All these new findings have led our team to conclude that the Hi-Line was not the simple, harmonious, sanguine place we painted it previously. Circumstances loomed there, and in the world, that would unnerve a yogi, that would drive a trucker to church, that would kill Saturday Night Live. And the news media, of course, capitalized on all of it, priming the pump of fear.

These days, by the time we walkers reached Hi-Line places, our nerves were shot. We wanted to be friendly, smile, and say "hi," but our minds were too noisy and our hearts too hardened with thoughts of the enemy or anticipation of war or economic disasters. We had to stay a few days to let the filtrate of doom settle, away from radio, TV, and print waves, and allow our hearts to soften and mellow like spring snow on a southern slope.

Signs of hope trickled through, though—hard data, really. More bicyclists, despite some renegades who defaced "No Biking" signs, pumping slowly up steep hills, looked up and "hi"-ed to hikers going down. And, in what might have been an aberration, just the other day a group of eight young men and women stopped their bantering, with one of them delivering a clear "hi" to a lone walker passing by. The walker, who happened to be this researcher, couldn't believe his ears and wasn't able to respond until several steps later. This event might be a sign pointing to a friendlier trend as people begin to realize, despite what the media would have us believe, their inbred peacefulness and good nature.

Another conclusion is that all this wariness heightened the need for Hi-Line protection, and so we've started Friends of the Hi-Line, a more-than-advocacy organization that will actually be fielding political candidates. Our intent will be nothing less significant than world peace, since anything else will disturb the sanctity and affability of Hi-Line situations. Our recent mission statement came out squarely against greed, hatred, and delusion and was in favor of peace, love, and cooperation.

We will not expect "hi"s all the time. People have their individual rights to pass by, eyes fixed on the ground ahead, legs churning like race horses, arms tucked up and in for speed, totally ignoring any human or other beings as they check their pulse watches and rush to return to safe, antiseptic territory inside their cars.

We *will* push for a peaceful world, though, where humans can begin to drop their suspicions of each other, where the first thought upon meeting is one of welcome, where a smile begins to form just about automatically and "hi"s burst spontaneously from both parties meeting, whatever the numbers, combinations, or permutations.

Remember, Vote Friends of the Hi-Line.

*STEPHEN ALTSCHULER*

# 36 URBAN WILDLIFE

*It became clearer to me, as life progressed, that finding natural places within the city was not just a matter of recreation but of emotional and spiritual survival. In the woods, finding nature meant stepping out of my door. But in the city, I needed to seek out these places and the wildlife that lived there.*

*In those wild places, something basic began to sink in: that acting from my gut would lead me to wholeness—would allow me to clear out of my own way and drop that mind that feared.*

*A blue jay feather picked up in the hills during my perambulations marked that insight in my journal. In the middle of my emotional storms, the quiet presence of wildlife living in and around the city restored my inner balance and provided sustenance to my spirit.*

It might sound incongruous, but this urban dweller needed wildlife more than he needed any so-called utility. No, the absence of wildlife in the area would probably not be a threat to human survival, but given the frenetic, jangled nature of the man-made world, the thought that wild animals roamed throughout the hills, living the simplest, most natural lives imaginable, healed and em-powered me. They ate mostly what they found that day, except for the vegetarians, who saved a few goodies for later. If their homes collapsed, they found others. If some external force threatened their well-being, they hid until the danger passed, then went on as if nothing ever happened. If they felt hot, they found shade. If thirsty, they found water. They might not have fun, in a human sense, but they also didn't sit around wondering if they were having it or not, as humans did. They didn't waste time, nor did they check the time, nor did they worry about being on time. They *were* time, in that their own bodies and brains served also as their clocks.

While I agonized between fettucini Alfredo or eggplant Par-mesan, wild animals had already eaten their supper and gone to sleep—without any TV, without any phone conversations with friends, without, even, a nighttime snack. And they didn't get up two hours later remembering they hadn't paid the utility bill.

Some might say, "How can you compare the way wild animals live and the way humans live?" And it was true: we had these opposable thumbs, and a cerebral cortex, and an upright spine, and rent to pay every month. But on the other hand, all of us mammals had two eyes, one nose, one mouth, two ears, appendages for locomotion and for making or suckling babies, lungs that breathed the same air, and an appetite. We had feelings and spirit, too, that kept us alive, let us feel fear, sense danger, realize safety, know those who are related to us, care for our offspring, feel pain, feel well-being, enjoy the warmth of the sun, and seek shelter from the rain. All mammals shared these characteristics.

We could easily see, then, wild animals as our brothers and sisters. We were attuned and attendant to each other. We had paid, therefore, and do pay now, a great psychic price for killing and harassing them. Our collective wounds dug deeply, as we grieved on fathomless, unknown levels for the grizzly bear, the kit fox, the cougar, the buffalo, the pronghorn, the condor, the Coho salmon, the wolf, the coyote, the fox, and the whale. We didn't even know how much we grieved, but our spiritually desolate lives reflected, and continue to reflect, the grief. We consoled ourselves by writing them off as just wild, untamed animals, unworthy of human compassion, care, and concern. We assuaged our guilt with rationales that separated us from their world, a world we referred to as so many habitats. Yet their world was our world. Their earth was our earth. Their habitat was our habitat.

Yet these are just words. Behind them, beside them, tears bear witness to a deep pain felt over the onslaught of wildlife. We have run roughshod over nature—a monstrous injustice—and although none of us wants to admit it, we are all accomplices of sorts.

Recently, while I was walking the East Bay hills, an owl's hoot greeted me, and I returned the call. The owl answered back in the fading twilight that separated two worlds. A moment suspended in time filled with kinship, understanding, and communication. Suddenly, the owl swooped down and flew near, as if to acknowledge our inherent camaraderie, since then remaining for me a reminder of kinship of other forms of life on this earth.

I needed wildlife, and not just on Sierra Club calendars or in coffee-table books. I needed wild beings to be there, living simply, with their own brand of dignity on this planet that served as their—our—hearth, host, and home.

# CREEK WALKING

In August I went to a Buddhist monastery in the Santa Cruz Mountains to the south and meditated for a week in a tent. Except for brief walks and the customary one meal a day, all I did was sit, in silence, and for seven days watch the day turn into night, just noticing the subtle changes inside and out. The Buddhists call this Dhutanga practice, or meditating on nature. Seeing life in this basic and powerful way reduced it to its lowest common denominator. In the tent I wrote: "Be a fool! Be a fool! Iron man, grab hold the mind and be a fool. Grab hold of the mind and settle the issue immediately. Directly seizing supreme enlightenment, don't concern yourself at all with right and wrong."

As I left the monastery, I told myself, "Now the real practice begins." For the world held fewer checks and balances to control a ram-

*paging, thinking mind that kept up an almost constant internal monologue. The stimuli of the city, along with inner doubts, made it likely I would forget the basics of living I'd experienced on the peaceful retreat. But I did have a way to remind myself of what was important, to remind myself of a bigger picture beyond the small, insular mind. That way involved walking.*

*Walking in nature added more to the spiritual pot than to the cognitive, and there everything seemed in place. So I trekked often to creeks, waterfalls, and parks within the city. At least there, I could relax in the present and renew my relationship with my own breath.*

Through walking about, I saw that creeks created the heart-blood of a town—arteries that descended from the hills, that greeted developed areas with the absolute trust common in the natural world. And the way a community returned the greeting measured its spirit. Did it slam the creek's doors with culverts, embalming its waters beneath concrete and asphalt? Did it bully the creek into back alleys, where it became little more than a cesspool? Or did the town showcase the creek, garnishing its banks with trees and flowers, embracing it and acknowledging the vital part it could play in people's lives?

Berkeley had several creeks still not fully encased by concrete. Capistrano, Codornices, Strawberry, Blackberry, Schoolhouse—the names danced with lightness, whimsy, and poetry.

A creek balanced the nature of a town. A creek had little to do with commerce or higher education or political leanings. It didn't try to better itself, for it had no self to better. It simply advanced: faster in wet weather, slower in dry. A creek modeled unity and simplicity, offering, to a frenetic town, relief from its willful activities.

*STEPHEN ALTSCHULER*

I've heard talk of breaking up some of the downtown parking lots that entomb Strawberry Creek—of resurrecting it and restoring it to its rightful place. If the creek were to flow downtown with renewed grace and grandeur, as it did on the university campus, it would nourish the soul of the town and the souls of all its inhabitants. At one time, as recently as 200 years ago, this area thrived as meadow and scattered woodland, filled with bunch grasses, clover, and coast live oak, its streams running into a much larger bay, its skies thick with migratory birds.

And, in deep ways, some of this natural beauty endured. A crust of concrete covered its surface, but if left unmaintained, even for as little as a hundred years, it would all return to the softness of soil, sand, and silt. The streets would heave and crack, and plant life and water would seep in, acidifying and decomposing the rock. Look at any abandoned parking lot and see oxalis and wild mustard at work creating a meadow for tomorrow.

It became clear to this creek walker that towns and cities needed to welcome the creeks back. We needed reminders of our own naturalness. We needed to see moving water with its places of stillness—places of quiet reflection within a form that changes constantly. We needed to have creeks close by, where we could see them, walk by them, smell the moisture, and touch the moss.

A human being, like a creek, moved, changed, flowed. A human being experienced eddies and swirls and waterspouts that felt, at times, as if they would suck us under. We experienced the still places, too, behind the stumps and rocks that felt so secure and safe, that felt so permanent. And we experienced the fast water, the white water, the floods that pushed the stumps and rocks aside, rearranging everything as we struggled and fought to keep it the same, lamenting our fate and sometimes cursing the forces that brought such calamity and upheaval. Even happiness led ultimately to sorrow, for its base was aversion to pain, and pain was an inevitable consequence of having a form, a body. Such happiness is ephemeral, although we wish, we pray, it would last as it begins to slip away.

A creek's life staged no such fight. In winter it ran full and fast. In summer it cut to a thin silver ribbon meandering along, letting gravity and the lowest places determine its course. A creek's life presented no problem to be solved or struggle to be overcome. It did not need to unfold or become. It showed no tension, no frustration, no anxiety, no expecting. Its water-course way took the path of least resistance in complete harmony with its earth-course way. The two interconnected: earth and water. And their union created a quality of harmony that made creek walking so appealing and nurturing.

In the hills above Berkeley courses a section of Wildcat Creek—a short stretch of wildness—that embraced, for me, the same spirit as the most awesome of any Sierra white water. Walking there quieted my busy mind. The imaginary line between "creek" and "self" dissolved. The walker just walked by water and woods, with no thought about them. The precipitate of mind settled, and the feet and eyes and ears took over. These sensors did not lie or deceive. They sensed with all their cells a certain holiness. They melded fervent activity and eternal stillness. They molded the nucleus of the soul.

In that moment of alternating quietness and excitement, love arose. It had always been there, but the sanctity of that mind state allowed love space to manifest. From that love an extraordinary moment surfaced, deep and expansive as an ancient lake, yet fleeting as a feather. Thought returned; the moment changed my insides. Like a great mother, the earth embraced, accepted, loved without condition.

Below the trail, water, unburdened by time, barreled through a gap in some large rocks. Soon, without ceremony, it would disappear underground on its run to the bay. Its spirit remained intact, though, and then, in that place, this creek awakened aliveness.

*STEPHEN ALTSCHULER*

# 38 MATTERS OF LIFE AND DEATH

*Spiritual practice taught me—perhaps its most important lesson—that things change. I think my grandmother told me that early on, but it took a great deal of experimenting with life before I started believing this obvious truth. It took fully feeling "the dark night of the soul," as the Christian mystics called the state of being in which you knelt at the bottom of the pit looking up without a hope of getting out, where the only things left to do were dig deeper or do nothing.*

*I didn't know if I hit the absolute bottom, but my view began to brighten as I continued to relate to nature (including people) in more honest, direct ways. I began to open more to my nature as well, and my spirit liked this. I felt the presence of a spiritual force in everything around me—trees, stones, birds, me, people—taking on different forms, dancing with it all.*

*Since September, my wife had been away on a second long-term meditation retreat, and I longed for the companionship provided by the institution of marriage. Now the time of her return approached, a change accompanied by happy, yet strangely uneasy, feelings—an uneasiness I didn't quite understand, manifested by a mild to medium anxiety in my head that usually meant I wasn't acknowledging some significant feeling. That feeling roiled between love, frustration, and confusion.*

*Emerging from retreats in the recent past, before coming to California, I had felt great inner power that gradually became diffuse and diluted as I muddled through several romantic relationships. And then a second marriage. Anticipating my wife's return, I told myself, "I need to rediscover that power within the form of this marriage. The Roshi (Zen Master) is before me."*

At thirty-eight I noticed the birth of a leaf for the first time. Growing up in a row-house East Coast city caused this omission in my early education. Before, there was winter and bare branches, and then suddenly a quick spring, followed by a long summer with trees adorned in fully mature leaves. For almost half a lifetime, one of the premier shows of nature had escaped my attention.

The birth of a flower blossom from its small bud, an event more obvious and eye-catching, did capture my attention. A leaf's bud, though, seemed less worthy to watch and, in comparison, dull: an ordinary green, miniature leaf curled up in fetal position, one day appearing in fullness. But a leaf has a flower, too—a very delicate flower, with all the accessories.

My discovery came from walking each day—a slowing down that revealed what had been in front of me for all those years. The wonder of it must have been what early human beings felt when they realized that making love led to babies. Before that awareness, as theorized by *Clan of the Cave Bear* author Jean Auel, they didn't link the two events. Since becoming aware of the birth of leaves I have never let another spring go by without spending time noticing deciduous trees and the cycle of their leaves.

Another event that for me had gone unnoticed was the actual moment a leaf left a tree in its fall to the ground at the end of the growing season. Millions of leaves had been falling, but never had I isolated in my awareness any one leaf's leaving the twig to which it had clung. The importance of this sighting had to do with missing another of nature's most significant events: the moment of the death of a leaf.

So the watching began, and it lasted a long time, focusing intently on one particular leaf, not knowing how long the release would take. An hour went by, then a second hour—a trance-like hour concentrating on that leaf. At times the distinction between leaf and self blurred. Scary stuff, losing boundaries, but the seeing provided the anchor to reality. We expend much creative energy maintaining such boundaries, on psychic, social, and national levels. For breaking the boundaries engendered thoughts of impending chaos, an image of falling apart and having no familiar land/self marks to call your own. Looking at that leaf flirted with those risky boundaries, but I resisted the self-preserving urge to cut and run.

Finally, without fanfare, the leaf fell, swirling to the ground. I rose slowly, never losing sight of it, and picked it up: a maple leaf, crinkled and brown, drained of life, dead, but somehow a part of the part of me that sees—the part that understands what it sees not in words but in feelings. That part remained alive regardless of circumstance, for in nature, its death would lead to life.

Humans are, of course, part of nature, but we have a much harder time accepting our death and seeing that it leads to, and makes way for, further life. Even with all the attention focused in recent years on death and dying, the issue is still circumvented widely by individuals, government leaders, and the medical establishment. Intellectually, we can see that if all of us went on living for ever and ever, eventually everyone and everything on the planet would become extinct. But emotionally, we generally deny the reality of death and insulate ourselves from its emergence into our consciousness. Every culture in history has had myths to explain death and to guide people through the experience itself and the thoughts about it. But the only mythology extant in this culture is the movies, where we see death and senseless violence, pinch ourselves that we are not on the screen, and then walk out very happy we are alive and won't have to go through what we witnessed. Or will we? The doubts linger, as we watch what happens to others on the evening news, and we fall asleep, literally and figuratively, with a residue of fear (that is, if we fall asleep at all, given the statistics on insomnia!).

So we need reminders, especially simple ones like the birth and death of a leaf, which are rarely reported on, and only a search of obscure poetry will reveal anything on the subject. But contemplating the life cycle of leaves offers a perspective on life not usually received from newspapers, books, or even an entire college education.

The leaf that fell that day gazes at me from its frame on my wall, and I look up at it often. It says, "STAY AWAKE!" It says, "Everything in nature is special and has something to teach." It says, "Here in death I am perfect as in life, a part of nature reflective of your true nature. And here in life I will help you remember . . . who you are, what you are doing here, what is important. I will help you remember that this life, in this moment, is connected to all life that has been, all life now alive, and all life that is to come. I will help you remember that birth and death come from the same breath, held together by tears of sorrow and joy."

*STEPHEN ALTSCHULER*

# MUD WALKING

In December the ground under my daily feet became much muddier as a fellow meditator unexpectedly called in a $4,000.00 loan he had extended to me a year before. I had used the money to live on while I thought through career decisions, but now I needed not so much a career but a job in order to pay him back by the time he requested. My inner child in this case was not wounded but spoiled, as I kicked and thrashed about, thinking of the prospect of having to take on a full-time job doing something I didn't want to be doing. Baby-boomers didn't like to be forced into something they didn't want to be doing, so I cried, overwhelmed by my panicky mind, in my wife's arms.

But, alas, I closed my eyes, opened my mouth anticipating the medicine, swallowed hard, and took a full-time job in a nursing home as an activities director, a job that pushed me physically, given the need to transport and arrange people in wheelchairs all day, and challenged me emotionally and spiritually, given the proximity to those same people, who were often suffering and dying. To prepare for the job I traveled to a Zen Center in the mountains east of Los Angeles to do sesshin (Japanese Zen retreat) with Sasaki Roshi, the powerful teacher I'd practiced meditation with before I moved to California.

The retreat and contact with this teacher brought enough power to deal fairly effectively with the job. But I had little or no energy left to be fully present in my marriage, and marriages required much energy. Sasaki Roshi wrote in his book, Buddha is the Center of Gravity (Lama Foundation, 1974): "When you hold your wife, you have to hold her with your whole being, otherwise you cannot make a good family . . . [W]hen you feel you cannot give yourself away, you should divorce. . . ."

So with the start of this job, the path of our marriage became rutted with one mud puddle after another, and although I eventually repaid my financial debt, emotionally I began slipping and sliding and teetering on the edge of falling.



I had a long and storied relationship with mud. That connection went back to early spring days, where on some forest roads in New Hampshire the only alternative to the muddy road was the forest thicket. There, such days were called spring, a name that I supposed was an attempt to lighten the burden of mud. Here in California, those wet days were called winter, or the rainy season, a name more in tune with the true nature of mud. There, mud jeopardized survival—newly transplanted emigrés from Boston would suddenly disappear, only to reappear on a hot, sticky summer day, wandering dazed down a dusty country road. Here, mud jeopardized nothing, since most people didn't have to go through it to get home, so they walked around it, or didn't walk at all. In California people could choose from a variety of options (indeed, a

Californian probably coined the word "options"). In New Hampshire, they pretty much had only one choice.

But I sought out mud here. It was harder to find, because a lot of walks were way up, then way down, so the rain drained too quickly for good, deep mud to develop. Berkeley had trails and undeveloped paths, though, where a rich base of mud had been churned in. This creation of mud is something we humans have really perfected. For nature itself didn't produce high-quality mud. Oh, occasionally a river bed might have some—though too solid, usually—and sometimes a swamp, on its way to meadow-hood, might have high mud content. But people or the animals most associated with people, like cows, dogs, and horses, made really good, slimy mud, mixing and churning and stirring, creating ridges and grooves and mini-mud canyons that challenged the best mud walkers around.

In fact, I was glad to see paleontologists corroborate this phenomenon when they found an ancient human footprint on the African tundra, preserved in lava mud, now dried and hardened. Even 10,000 or 15,000 years ago we were perfecting our mud-making abilities. If there had been a little water on the moon, Neil Armstrong would have walked, jumped, and driven through it, creating "one small step for man" and one giant mud puddle for mankind. I've never seen humans pass up an opportunity to make mud.

Now, this is not a criticism of our species, for mud can lead to metaphysical awakenings. It's the instability of mud, the uncertainty of it, that counts. Mud actually makes the ground move, and we like our ground to be solid. After all, mud is matter, and matter is supposed to be cohesive, with organized molecules holding it all together in orderly fashion. Walking on mud creates a whole new level of consciousness. No longer can we predict smugly that the earth will support us, will stay still, while we move about. For that reason, perhaps, Californians, for the most part, avoid mud. Earthquakes thoroughly satisfy any needs for terrestrial instability.

Adding to that instability is the tendency for mud to cake on the bottom of shoes, giving the feeling of walking on small rocks. The foot is separated from the ground by these clumps, which seem to grow like the Blob that ate some city in a Class C horror flick. And without the foot, or even the shoe, contacting the ground directly, the ego can begin to feel as if it were breaking apart. As Dr. Freud would have put it, the ego becomes threatened as the id receives more and more expression, and the superego, in the form of internalized parental voices, yells from the sideline, "Look at you! You're getting all muddy. Now get out of that puddle this instant!"

Mud is primal stuff, characterized by such words as *ooze, slime,* and *muck,* and rendering images of pigs, dirty little boys, and hippopotami. It's the opposite of the values on which our civilization is based: cleanliness, propriety, common sense, and order. But if we were to descend into mud, to wallow in it the way water buffaloes do in southeast Asian backyards, and to muck up our pores, hair, and fingernails, our culture might advance to higher levels instead of remaining in its present spiritual torpor. Mud might loosen us up, producing a kind of Woodstock in the nineties—kids, teens, moms, dads, chief executive officers all following their bliss, rolling in it. Yesterday, rock: today, mud. Freud would definitely have seen it as a vast pool of repressed sexual fantasy. And Californians, particularly those in southern California, so used to burbling about lounging *au naturel* in hot tubs, would, of course, lead the way, importing New Hampshire mud, creating Great MudAmerica or DisneyMudLand theme parks. Or northern Californians would no doubt find some therapeutic value for mud, perhaps reviving new-millenium versions of encounter mud groups or the har-mud-ic convergence, in which mud would be flung at each other or lovingly walked in, respectively.

Mud could be the missing link that could explain the Christian Science joke: "What is mind? No matter; What is matter? Never mind." The immediacy of mud forces a suspension of thinking. Facing mud, it's difficult to be egocentric and narcissistic. It's difficult to be preoccupied with the trivialities of vanity and jealousy. It's

*STEPHEN ALTSCHULER*

difficult to be stuck in our heads. Mud is wild and crazy stuff. But I digress: all I really want to describe is how to walk in mud.

Mud walking does involve a certain technique, one that allows for creativity and relative stability. It entails leaning backward slightly on the heels, keeping the arms buoyant and stretched like a tightrope walker's balancing pole, and fixing the eyes about four feet in front, scanning the frontier of the next step. You enter the mud more with your heart than feet, like a ninety-meter ski jumper preparing to fly. In mud, steps are not just steps but little adventures involving tiny slips and slides. Your internal navigator must make rapid adjustments, but, alas, mud is too changeable, too unpredictable for that gyroscope in the brain.

So, by walking in mud, we force an exploration of our limits. How far out of control will we allow ourselves to become? How close will we risk disaster, and do we somehow crave a crisis? Do we somehow, on some level, want to lose our ground and fall in the mud? Is there a three-year-old in all of us that wants to wallow, that wants to be totally covered in mud? And if an inner child in most of us needs to be healed, as the pop psychologists tell us, wouldn't mud be better, and more fun, and cheaper therapy than talking to a psychotherapist for umpteen Woody Allen years?

I've never fallen in a good mud puddle, nor have I walked barefoot in one—something that probably says something about my own inner child. I passed one fellow on an Oakland path, however, who was completely covered with mud and, along with his companion, was laughing and carrying on about it. The whole scene displayed a great advertisement for not getting too skilled at mud walking, for I envied the anarchy of the way he looked: totally out of control, yet laughing like a loon. I smiled and made some flip comment, but it was he who was really having fun with life. I remained an observer looking out from behind my mind. He embodied never-mind matter, which is what really matters. For the moment, he lost his mind in a very sane, sanguine sort of way, and that's what I always imagined spiritual enlightenment to be.

Compared to the riches of New Hampshire, California lacked much mud this year, but what little there was deepened my understanding of, and relationship with, mud (along with my love of the word *mud*, which I've just become aware of using in almost every sentence in this discourse). I needed to unlearn so much more, though. Next year I hope to loosen my technique a bit, perhaps reining in my balance-pole arms, allowing a fall, and lying there laughing. Maybe then, in full embrace, mud and I will marry, and I'll awaken to a life happily ever insecure.

*STEPHEN ALTSCHULER*

# WATCHING AND WALKING (IN THE FORM OF HIKING)

*In the summer of 1985, my debt repaid, I left my job at the nursing home and accompanied my wife to Thailand, at her request, to help her prepare for a three-month major-league meditation retreat in Burma. It didn't make much sense for me to go, considering my own needs, but, at this point within the marriage I continually forgot to consider my own needs.*

*So we went to, and survived the bacterial ravages of, Southeast Asia, and seemed to draw even further apart from each other. The Burmese Buddhist form she practiced was an ancient path supposedly first set forth by the Buddha, with rules prescribed for monks and nuns living in community (or Sangha) with each other. The Buddhist path offered total liberation from mental and physical suffering—a noble end that I supported wholeheartedly—but the means to get there involved* rigorous long-term meditation sitting still with a straight back, and limiting one's outward behavior by strictly structured precepts, which renunciates and, to a degree, lay practitioners, were required to follow. After eighteen months of working at a fairly exhausting full-time job, I was ready to bust out and felt constricted by those uncompromising, though worthwhile, social structures. So the nature of our needs polarized, and that polarization caused increased tension.

I didn't communicate this to her, but I felt suffocated by the spiritual path and its restrictions. At the time, I was reading Krishnamurti, the Indian teacher who advocated dropping all forms of religious dogma and discovering the truth for oneself. The two approaches to self-understanding may have had similar ends, but the means were as different as Apples and IBMs. I kept quiet—a major fault of mine—for fear of rocking the marital boat.

So she went into deep monastic retreat, and I returned alone to the United States in August to a small cabin in Mendocino County for a month-long retreat of my own design. All the feelings I'd bottled up came out as I wrote in my journal and watched the days become night high above the coastal fog to the west.

My retreat was truly a benediction, for in the process of self-examination I got clearer as to what I wanted. The effects were explosive, and I emerged with hope . . . and fear—fear of opening lines of communications that I suspected would smash the marriage to smithereens. I was to be right about that, but it wouldn't happen for another three years.

In October I went back to the Mendocino cabin to celebrate my fortieth birthday alone, my wife still in Burma. It was cooler then, and I was wiser, as I watched and walked and did some hard hiking.

STEPHEN ALTSCHULER

# WATCHING

In late fall, at the small Mendocino cabin that reminds me of my former New Hampshire home, it is colder. The wind bites at my flesh. Yet that wind is still so yielding, so soft and giving. I return to a place where I had unburdened myself of many mind rocks, where I had watched my own mind change and develop with the days. I am not there to try to repeat the experience, for each dance is different, with a new configuration, a new set of circumstances and conditions. I am there to celebrate an emergence. To celebrate that silence that comes with seeing. Yes, my mind is quieter, does not move as much with all the worldly changes, is more sensitive and awed by life in all its forms.

On the first day back I go to a special spot on the ridge where someone had built a bench facing west. The sun nears the horizon. It is further south than in August and sets much earlier. The sky is still dominated by blues—three or four hues. That soft, ethereal, misty light so special to California. The winds begin to subside. Since I am finally far enough from the highway, the quiet deepens. The space between the two worlds of day and night narrows. My mind stills, settling after the doings of the day—the getting there.

In a few moments the sun is gone from sight. The valley below is muted, smoky with dusk. The sky is like the pre-dawn I saw that morning in the hills above Berkeley, and the air is just as nip. Where is the time between dawn and dusk? Only clocks announce the time, and human beings make the clocks. So I suppose it's human beings who make time. And I suppose if I am counting birthdays, I am making time along with the rest.

Now, the earth is lover, cradled in my arms,
naked, uncovered, soft and warm.
No longer Mother, but sensuous,
As she gives without wanting,
offers without asking,

like a blush young maiden,
her eyes closed,
ready for her first kiss.

With the sun gone, the sky fills with orange hues. A glow
where the sun was, then amber, then slate blue, almost purple. The
evergreens breathe easy before winter storms descend. The wind is
suddenly turbulent, as if pestered by some unseen force, sending
through the trees a murmur that borders on a groan. I've heard that
wind before in the New Hampshire cabin. I've taken some giant
steps in the years in between, each one necessary for the next.

With nightfall my body tires. It has been a full day. A fortieth
birthday. The pines sway easily, like chanting monks, against the
mauve sky. One last look, then my eyes close softly, easing carefully
down the fullness they feel.


# WALKING
# (IN THE FORM OF HIKING)

I hate to hike. I mean, I love to hike, but after the love of
hiking gets me to the trail, I hate to hike. I mean, I love to hike,
but when heart is pounding, ascending a hill, and legs are heading
for hell, and mind is fixed only on the hill's top and its subsequent
leveling off and descent, I hate to hike.

I really love to hike when I've been sitting inside for a lifetime
of Monday mornings and the wind has blown away the smog and
I can see the mountains across the bay as clean as glacial ice. Such
conditions herald a hike, and visions of the way it will be dance in
my head like the Sirens that tempted Ulysses. The legs begin to
sense it first and then get up, often for the most ridiculous reasons.
Then the arms move, almost uncontrollably, and the head turns to
the outside as a compass needle turns north. Like an addict, I am

*STEPHEN ALTSCHULER*

hooked, not on the hike itself but the thought of it. And like the actions of the addict, the thought and the event are inseparable.

So I go. It is not even a conscious decision. I do not say *Should I?* or *Shouldn't I?* The lure of the hike is like a beautiful woman beckoning me. I do not hesitate but rush headlong into her wanting arms. She envelops me with kisses and hugs as we make love till dawn, and we lie there exhausted, not even knowing each other's names. And as it would be with such a woman, I consider nothing of the consequences, of the potential pain of succumbing totally to my sensory desires.

I go: to the hills, the mountains, the beach, the steep, Bay Area public pathways and stairways—it doesn't really matter. The itch and the urge must be satisfied. How good it feels to scratch, but how irritated if I scratch too hard!

Ultimately, though, I love to hike, and if I could hike always on an ultimate plane of existence, I would be in eternal bliss. But this body aches so at times, and this mind hates the aching. Yet what can I do? These legs will not stop. These eyes will not close. This walker's soul will not rest, although at times—upon a time, for a time, in time, because of time, despite, in nirvana, there being no time—this body hates to hike and would be done with it if this mind and spirit didn't love it so.

# WILD AND SOLO
# THINGS

In the early winter I had bought a ticket for a week-long
retreat to be held in May with Krishnamurti at his American headquar-
ters in Ojai, California. His books and tapes were having a profound
effect on me, expanding my view of meditation as a vehicle for exploring
the origins of thought, the origins of ego, the origins of suffering. I had
years before seen and heard him speak, considering him a provocative
thinker but essentially an iconoclast who devalued all reliance on reli-
gion or any meditation techniques. But as is often the case, when I
reread some of his books as an older and more evolved reader, his message came through in much different ways. At ninety-or-so years old,
Krishnamurti was reportedly in failing health, so this week with him
promised to be a rare, and perhaps final, opportunity to be in his pres-

ence. On February 17, however, a few months before the scheduled retreat, Krishnamurti died.

With a mid-life crisis gathering steam, I felt a bit lost for a time after that, and within two months I sank into a sizable depression. I withdrew into self-absorption, which did not do good things for my marriage. Somewhat desperate and lacking any direction, I entered psychotherapy and tried to bolster myself as well with what I'd learned from spiritual practice.

Nearly broke, I teetered vulnerably on and sometimes over the edge of tears. I had flight fantasies, imagining running away—from everything. I knew the tense, tight anxiety in my chest would follow me, though. I felt fear, but I wasn't exactly sure of what.

I sojourned to Ojai anyway that May, since the organizers went ahead with the planned week, playing Krishnamurti videos and holding discussions led by some of his long-time associates (he discouraged people becoming disciples or students and appointed no successor to continue his teachings). Sipping tea in a Forest Service campground fifteen miles from Ojai, I reflected, after the first day, on one of Krishnamurti's teachings that said: if your life is a mess, change it. Think clearly. He also said, know the mess, be with it, feel it, observe it, and therein lies the most dynamic action.

Thus fortified, and fully supplied with tent, sleeping bag, and a sense of humor (the main ingredient for surviving my mid-life crisis), I embarked the next month on my first solo backpacking trip into the wilds of the Sierra Nevada. It was a good classroom, because all the basics of life emerged, and every moment tested what I'd learned.

Recently, in Sequoia National Park, I saw a mama bear with two cubs trailing close behind, all climbing a wild, wooded hill. A beautiful and memorable sight, but weren't bears dangerous? Indeed

*STEPHEN ALTSCHULER*

they were, a Ranger warned. Don't approach them too closely, especially when cubs are present. Hang your food in a tree in camp. If they come poking around, or if you surprise one on the trail, bang pots together to drive them off. Wear bells on your shoes. Same with snakes, frowned the Ranger. Read the warning signs. Rattlers were out sunning themselves on the trails. Watch at least four feet ahead. Don't approach closely. Keep your tent closed at all times. And ticks—the area is infested with them. Ticks carry something called Lyme disease. Rangers have already been stricken. The head honcho in Washington got arthritis at thirty-five after being bitten by a tick in the Everglades. Very dangerous. Keep your pants tucked in your socks. Stay on the trail. Wear light-colored clothes.

Now, these were helpful suggestions, and had, I was sure, prevented many mishaps and serious injuries. But the next day, near a campground, I saw another bear who wasted no time in running away when he saw me. My conditioning told me the bear would attack and not run, but the bear must have talked to one too many Rangers.

Even before hearing the wary Ranger's admonitions, I equated wilderness (which originally was defined as anything outside my playpen) with danger, and danger was to be avoided. In previous years I had done my share of backpacking and botanizing but had never gone into the wilderness alone. Even my stay in the New Hampshire woodland cabin was on the relatively safe side, and I never ventured far beyond the security of hearth and home. Fear stopped me, fear of the unknown, of all the anticipated disasters brought to term by catastrophic thinking—thinking honed by years of wincing from a mother's worry and the relentless barrage of TV and radio news reports.

So it was in that frame of mind, along with a deepening depression that needed some wilderness as an antidote, that I decided to go on my first solo backpacking trip—not in the relatively tame East, where I had lived most of my adult life, but in the wild open spaces of the western mountains: in the high Sierra with its old-growth evergreen forests and glacial moraines crawling with man-eating bears, rattlesnakes, mountain lions, howling coyotes, Lyme-diseased ticks, and a sun so bright with UV-A and UV-B rays zapping through the thin, high mountain air that my fair skin would instantly erupt with tumors and pustules. To daunt me further, every backpack guidebook I read advised against hiking alone, espousing worst-case scenarios the way a TV evangelist invokes the hellish consequences of sin.

The warnings came too late, though. I had already told all my friends I was going, although I did consider faking the whole expedition. Honesty prevailed, however. Shadows had to be faced. Darth vaders and alma maters and various poxes of the spirit had to be reckoned with. The wild called out to me, and this chicken could find no place left in the coop to hide.

And what a strong voice the wild had, to overcome the conditioning voices of fear! With mere whispers, birdsong, and tiny cricket feet it beckoned. Why did I trust this voice when I distrusted so many other human voices? Why did I seek out this voice and listen so intently to the spirit of its message? Why could I understand it although it used no words? There must have been something primal in that voice, something before birth that lay like a seed waiting for acknowledgement.

It said *Come to the wilderness,* so I listened and did; and on Day One, to get used to the altitude and try out my new tent before hitting the trail, I checked into a campground. All was smooth until early the next morning about 4:00 A.M. I heard the first raindrops—more voices of the wild—but my conditioning got the better of me. I got up, packed the tent so it wouldn't be wet for the trip (but weren't tents supposed to get wet?), and sat in my car for the next four hours, a prisoner of the heavy rain and my even heavier worrying mind. The rain got harder, continuing as the light brightened. I couldn't hike in this weather. I'd . . . God forbid (again, my mother's voice) . . . get wet. I didn't have Gore-tex. How could I hike in the rain without Gore-tex? How *did* the old timers—the old Sierra Club founders—hike before Gore-tex? I was sure the wet wild was waiting to swallow whole my Gore-tex-less body.

I didn't have a self-inflatable mattress, either. I would probably freeze in the subalpine spring. The Ranger at the visitors' center said I would have to ford several creeks on this hike, and . . . how did she put it? . . . "The water is running really fast right now, and *is it* cold! Be careful. It could be very dangerous." Hey, no problem. I jumped many a South Philadelphia puddle when I was a kid. What's a little ole wild Sierra man-eating creek?

But as weather will do, it showed signs of clearing, and my excuses were running out. I drove to the trailhead, got my pack together, and headed out with about sixty pounds on my back, thirty of which was food. And, too, as weather will do, it started once again to rain . . . hard. The wild was heavy on my heels, and winning. If a bear appeared then, the Rangers wouldn't have much difficulty finding it: they could just look for the Camp Trails label on the backpack it'd be carrying.

With the fog obliterating any scenery (and three days later, on the way out, I saw how spectacular it was), I was hiking for hiking's sake. This was destination hiking, counting every step in units of mouthfuls of anticipatory dinner and moments of rest upon reaching a campsite. Two hikers looking weather-weary approached from the opposite direction.

"You like this?" asked the young European woman hiking out with her man friend, both obviously wishing they were back at a quiet cafe in Amsterdam, sipping *koffie met schlag*.

"Well, it's an experience," I replied, sounding very Californian. No, I didn't particularly like it, and when the wind blew my poncho up and over my head, exposing my pack and wetting my sleeping bag, I contemplated making camp right there on the three-foot-wide trail. Then, thirty seconds after the two people were on their way, the straps holding my bag and sleeping pad let loose, the whole deal coming within inches of falling about 300 feet into the raging Middle Fork of the Kaweah River below.

That near-accident marked a low point in my nascent solo backpacking career, although I was thankful that nobody saw it save my spirit guides and other universal forces, who were probably now laughing so hard they were about to fall off a cloud. Non-physical as they were, I was spared hearing their guffaws, however.

As with many low points, though, it also marked a turning point. I took a moment to assess the situation. The merciful gods must have taken pity, for the rain seemed to lighten as they sensed a sincere man, a humble man, really, a believer of sorts, about to break and run. End of severe test. Even Job eventually got a break.

Okay, I'm okay. No problem. Just re-strap it all together, and be off. The couple had said the first campsite was only about a half-mile away. Piece of cake. And step by step I was discovering that I could take care of myself, that F.D.R.—that blessed presidential metaphysician—was right about fear after all: beyond fear itself, there is nothing to fear.

The couple must have been itching to get out, for the half-mile turned out to be a mile and a half. But I finally eased down my pack, put up my tent next to a raging Panther Creek, and munched down about ten pounds of trail mix. No problem. It was almost as if the arduous hike had never happened as my hand automatically dipped into the gorp bag and up to my mouth, chewing, chewing, swallowing, dipping, feeling and grasping, particularly, for the chocolate chips.

F.D.R. notwithstanding, lingering fears did creep back into consciousness as the evening wore on, even without the evening news to stir things up. Had I strung the food high enough in the tree to keep bears from standing on their tippytoes to snare it or sending a cub out on the limb to hoist it up? The literature seemed to indicate that bears had more than borderline I.Q.s and were holed up in their dens with topo maps and cellular field phones.

And water fears: Rangers, books, and outdoor stores made it sound as if all the pollutants of the Western Hemisphere had drained into these mountain waters. The protozoa *Giardia lamblia*—the name sounds like a Mafia hit man with a lisp—was in there waiting, waiting for some thirsty human to dip in his Sierra cup and slurp and guzzle . . . and die. Water fears brought back memories of old Lone Ranger shows in which the masked man and Tonto find a skull next to a desert water hole, and Tonto goes "Hm, Kemosabe. This water bad."

And me, bigshot, decided to buy this cutting-edge water purification system, of which the guy at the store says, "I don't know. I haven't tried it. Looks like it'd work, though."

Yes, there were fears beyond fear itself. But I finally purified the water, cooked a simple dinner of tea and trail mix, and crawled into my cozy tent with a copy of *The Tracker*, a flashlight, a bottle of water, and . . . damn! four sticks of chewing gum that filled the tent, and probably the entire canyon of the Kaweah, including the bear dens, where odor sensors were spiking, with the scent of sweet, luscious peppermint. The bear bags were up, my boots were wet, but I'd have to do something. Images of bears sitting in my tent chewing gum came to mind, images that were parts of some *Life in Hell* or *Far Side* cartoon. I'd have to bury the gum, so I got out and did.

Later, when I opened my eyes after falling asleep, I was surprised to see that it was still dark. It felt as if I had slept through the whole night, but the clock showed only 1:30 A.M. I shook it and checked to see if the second hand was moving. 1:31 A.M. A long night ahead. So I picked up *The Tracker* and started to read a chapter about Tom Brown's harrowing experience with wild dogs in the Jersey Pine Barrens. Definitely the wrong chapter to read on a first solo wilderness backpack. By the end of the chapter I had lit the candle lantern as well and was wide-eyed. And the time, which felt as if it should have been at least 5:55 A.M., read 1:54 A.M. At least, Panther Creek was close enough and loud enough to drown

out the sound of bears, bobcats, and cougars more than likely tear-
ing, ripping, and snarling over my food bags.

Eventually, as nights will do, it ended, and the tent gradually
lightened as dawn approached. I emerged like an Argonaut buoyed
by a Golden Fleece sun. Amazing what the sun can do for one's
mood—how it burns away fear, adds hope, and turns shy people
into tigers. It, too, has a voice that soothes and caresses like a
lover's. To my amazement the food bags survived the night, dangling
from the tree the way Tom Dooley did but still alive and very much
intact. I could see the bears scratching their heads the way Stan
Laurel did.

I laid everything out on the rock exposed to the sun, including
myself, to bask in its warmth and nurturance. The admonishing
voices of the past grew dimmer as I breathed with a new-found
confidence. I had met the enemy and somehow managed to find a
pair of dry socks to put on him.

That day I trekked deeper into the wilderness, then stayed two
more nights, returning on the fourth day with a lighter pack and
lighter, more vital, mind and heart. At the end of that five-mile hike
gushed a fabulous waterfall, and I immediately thought of stripping
and submerging my sweaty body under the roaring falls. So, without
any further thinking, I did, screaming as the ice-cold water crashed
over me. If I thought then of the possibility of dying of shock, as
a friend later warned could have happened, I would have gotten
entangled in my usual mental webs of decision-making and never
felt the exhilarating water. But here, alone, with no one to speak
of the dangers, I let my gut guide me, and . . . Oh, how glorious
that cold dive was! Not only did it wash me clean and refreshed,
but it washed away the last of the fears of this solo trip. Not only
was the wild less dangerous than I thought, but I was more a friend
to myself than the critical judge I had been.

So, soon after, I began to plan a return trip, this time without
worry. Bring on the bears, bring on the ticks (a Ranger had to dig
two out of me after the first trip), bring on the rain and spooky

sounds in the night, bring on the mind—that *maitre d'* of fear, that impresario of trauma, that fabricator of thanatological thought. I will pack survival cards, first-aid kit, New-Age affirmations, and granola and chocolate chips mixed in a fifty-fifty ratio. All ready to re-enter nature, marching to her voice that muted the inner voices of anticipatory fear and acknowledging that the wild is a friend. The wild is a friend. The wild is a friend. The wild is a. . . .

# MONKEY TRAP MIND

In the middle of my money problems and stagnant career
plans, near the bottom of an emotional well, I was chosen, late in 1987,
to be a salaried staff writer for a group that was doing a book on
cancer, with me given the assignment of focusing on the psychosocial
aspects. Although I considered myself a capable writer, since 300 appli-
cants had competed for only three positions I felt that the hand of God
had just reached down and lifted me to Olympus. It was a dream
job—decent money, meaningful work, part-time so I could pursue other
writing projects, and the luxury of setting up shop whenever and wherever I wanted, including Point Reyes National Seashore to the west,
where, with a newly-purchased laptop computer, I wrote often.

It was a turning point, in terms of career and marriage. The job
gave me strength and an affirmation that I was a more capable human
being than my marriage led me to believe. And that marriage became a

power struggle, on the order of Armageddon, as I sought ways to free up and express what boiled in me.

As a husband and lover, I kept so much inside. I was not giving. I was withholding. I withheld truth. And therein stemmed the source of my pain. I felt a great sadness.

I did not especially like being married. Physically, I was not alone; emotionally, I was. I had put on a show for a long time, long before this marriage, back into my childhood. I had hidden from my family, embarrassed, ashamed, to be or reveal myself. A hole formed. And I had been trying to fill it with love ever since. But I hadn't a notion how to return any love I received. My cold hands mirrored my cold heart. I became very tired of playing husband and not doing a very good job of it. And yet it was not time to leave. I needed to stay and understand myself and this marriage more. Accepting this was difficult, and I wanted to be alone at this time. I would, however, let events take their course.

The marriage had become a monkey trap of sorts, but it took a physical injury from another form of the trap to get me to see how my mind had dulled through indulgence in emotional withdrawal.

The fall happened in late October at Tuolumne Meadows in Yosemite high Sierra country, a place that sounds odd for a fall, because the thought of falling from a meadow doesn't conjure images of catastrophe. Snow would soon close the road, making this the last weekend this part of the park would be accessible by automobile.

I went to camp and hike with good buddy Bob, an old friend from New Hampshire who had also moved to California. We planned it as a men's weekend out, to escape the pressures of the

*STEPHEN ALTSCHULER*

city, remember old times, and create new memories with some anticipated off-trail adventures.

We arrived late on a Friday, set up camp in the megalopolis campground, got a good night's sleep, and arose at the crack of noon to begin our trek into even higher country. High puffball clouds, clear views, snow-capped distant peaks, and moderate temperatures made a near-perfect setting. A great day for a hike . . . so we thought. Doesn't it always seem as if it'll be great at the start of such ventures? Full of hopes of things to see, hear, feel. Expectations of spiritual awakenings nurtured by the quiet of the mountains and high plateaus, letting the dust of the city waft away, replaced with the clean, fresh, rich air of the untrammeled Yosemite. Sort of a John Muir state of mind.

So we set off, like dancers in time with the timeless wilderness. And we stayed in time throughout the day, hiking cross-country, climbing a peak off-trail, discovering a high mountain pond, and eating lunch while basking in the Range of Light.

As the light began to wane, we headed back, intoxicated with peacefulness, to a friendly campsite and a good meal by the fire. As we neared the campground, though, the thought of firewood entered our heads, remembering that the campsite area had been stripped of dead wood for a quarter-mile around. We would have to find a large dead tree and haul it almost a half-mile . . . and we did. No problem for a couple of urban backwoodsmen.

"Okay, we'll need some kindling, too," yelled Bob, after we'd heaved down the heavy timber. "Here, help me pull this branch down."

Whereupon I leapt upon a huge boulder (another Muir moment), grabbed the seemingly-dead branch, and jumped down still clutching the bowed bough as if it were a matter of life and death. I waited for it to crack and break under the mighty pressure I was applying. No go, so I pulled harder . . . and harder. Still no go, and the thought occurred at that moment to let go. Just let go, and be done with it. The branch won this round. Nature had again proved mightier than man. There were some things we could not conquer, and we must accept this and allow the forces of nature to rule as they did for eons before humankind arrived.

But, no, this stubborn outdoorsman refused to submit so quickly to the power of Mother Nature. He had to uphold the heritage and reputation of his father, Big Mo (as his South Philly cronies called him, acknowledging in a word his head, height, and heart). Big Mo had been dead for almost two years, but there was a lot of Big Mo in Not-Quite-So-Big Stephen. Big Mo would never have given in to Nature. He would have pulled and pulled, like a bulldog, until either he or "the goddamn tree" (his probable words) came crashing down. An intractable optimist, he would never have admitted defeat, and although his son had only a fraction of Big Mo's tenacity, he, too, would not let go.

Even with antidotal Zen training, Gestalt therapy, blessings from several channeled, non-physical entities, and knowledge of the South American monkey trap, I, with my smarter friend standing by urging me on but not touching the branch himself, vaulted up to try to bring the consecrated kindling down with the weight of my body—non-existent in its essence, as some Eastern gurus claimed.

Now, you may be wondering what a monkey trap has to do with this, and for those who have never heard of this lo-tech, but very effective, device, let me explain. A gourd with an opening at one end is baited with a chunk of food, then tethered to and suspended from a tree. Monkey comes along, puts hand in gourd, grabs food, and tries to pull hand out to eat food. The hole in the gourd is now, however, too small for the monkey to pull out its clenched fist filled with food. Monkey hunter comes by and slips captured monkey into sack. But why, you ask, doesn't the monkey just let go of the food and pull out its hand, now unclenched and easily removed from the opening in the gourd? Why, indeed. The monkey has only one thing in mind: the food in its hand, and will not let

*STEPHEN ALTSCHULER*

go even as the hunter approaches. The trap is not only the gourd, but the monkey's own mind, fueled by its desires and attachments.

Are you getting the picture? All this slightly-more-advanced monkey had to do was let go of the branch, let go of my stubborn determination—a form of greed, actually—and all would've have been as it was before: that is, my body in healthy condition, out looking for fallen kindling. But as I jumped, my feet and legs flailed out horizontally, launched by the taut and coiled branch, and, pushed to the point of chaos, the branch broke with this six-foot, one-inch, 180-pound body falling several feet like Humpty Dumpty, hitting the solid, rock-strewn ground, crushing all the king's horses and all the king's men, along with the fourth lumbar vertebra. As a five-year-old once told me, "Pain hurts"—wisdom I never completely understood until that moment.

I'd been caught in the monkey trap of my mind. I wouldn't let go. Knowing on some level that the dangers far outweighed the benefits of breaking that branch, I wouldn't let go. And the results were catastrophic. I lay there winded, wondering if I'd done permanent damage. Bob told me later that I'd missed hitting my head on a rock by less than an inch. Had I hit it, I would surely have been knocked out and probably hospitalized.

Still, something in me said I'd never be quite the same. Neither paralyzed nor writhing in pain, my body was different, however, out of line, traumatized. I'd crossed a boundary line of sorts, for at forty-two I sensed that for the first time I'd broken a part of my body. I didn't know if my back was broken, but I, in a general sense, felt broken, incapacitated . . . and a bit embarrassed, as some nearby campers glanced over, bemused.

I looked up at Bob, who asked how I was, and wanted to say, "Fine, no problem. Let's get the fire started." But I could say nothing except a weak, "I don't know," through my scant breath. I didn't want to believe this happened. Then I tried to get up and the denial ended.

This was no simple injury. I couldn't just walk it off the way a young jock walked away on a twisted ankle. In fact, walking flashed into my mind. Would I be able to walk as before? An important question for one who made part of his living walking and writing essays on the subject.

Later, my injury was diagnosed, after x-rays, as a compression fracture of the fourth lumbar vertebra. Nothing requiring a brace or surgery, but it inflamed a whole skein of upper-back muscles and tendons involved in lifting and pulling, and, although the nerves were not pinched, they knotted into a malformed mass, twisted like the front end of a car after a crash. I was unable to do what I could normally do, and my body had never experienced that. In fact, I had felt in better shape at that time than at twenty-five. But after this personal Jericho, my perception of myself changed. I continued to be in relatively good shape, but now, finally, I could no longer delude myself into believing I was a young man. My definition of "normal" needed to change or be thrown out entirely.

As I soon discovered, I could still walk, but after a few miles, or if I stood still too long, my body would start to feel as if knuckles dug into my upper back. A knot of pain accompanied me almost constantly, with the hardest position being lying on a bed trying to fall asleep—a condition usually associated with the alleviation of pain. Everything I did, everywhere I turned, I was reminded of the fall and the monkey trap I'd been caught in.

How many more times in this life would I reach into the trap, grab the figurative food, and not let go, incarcerating myself in a prison of my own making? Why did I do such things? Was I not a free man? Or was I no different from a laboratory rat, prodded and tortured this way and that? Was I not in control of my life, my mind? Apparently not—at least, not as much as I thought.

In that instant, holding the bent branch I had transformed into a potentially lethal catapult, I was unconscious, and, for all intents and purposes, dead. An inner wisdom knew I should let go, be at

*STEPHEN ALTSCHULER*

peace. But a black shroud covered that wisdom as I staggered, intoxicated by 100-proof ego. I can do it, I thought. I won't be hurt. I am mightier than this tree. I will have my kindling. I will. I will. I will.

I will. There's been a lot of deviation in the way "I will" is used. "I will" has created Sistine Chapel frescoes and the depletion of the ozone layer. "I will" brought indoor plumbing as well as shopping malls built on filled-in wetlands. My own "I will" wrote many published articles but then would not permit me exit from the monkey trap. And my will was nothing other than me, so I couldn't shift the responsibility to early socialization or public school or the devil . . . or God, for that matter. The responsibility for getting into the trap, for the way I used "I will," fell on me, and the way out of the trap was just as obvious.

Just let go . . . of all I imagined necessary for happiness . . . of wanting everything to go my way . . . of ideas of life . . . of self and will . . . and pine branches—real and figurative—that wouldn't break. To be a full, alive, realized human being, I didn't need any of that.


It's been six months, and I have not fallen again. I have been walking, swimming, and avoiding all lifting and pulling. Try not lifting for even six hours: it's not easy, considering groceries and laundry, and considering today, when I shouldn't have carried a flat tire to the garage for repair but did and re-stretched some of those aforementioned muscles and tendons. The back is sore again and tight . . . again the result of the monkey trap and my tendency to stick my hand in and not let go. I could have found another way with the tire . . . like getting help.

I will not hang onto trees again but, I'm sure, will put my hand into another monkey trap, baited with something I want. I will again wobble at the edge of consciousness, needing only to open my eyes and hand to be free. The Venerable Thich Nhat Hanh once wrote: "The secret of meditation is to be conscious of each second of your existence and to keep the sun of awareness continually shining . . . in all circumstances, on each thing that arises." Maybe I should have that tattooed on the back of my hand.

# 43   COYOTE

Between April and July, 1988, my marriage began crumbling apart. My wife and I had purchased a house the previous year, but rather than being a source of joy, it just added to my pressures. And we were not communicating very well with each other.

I realized, after much soul searching, that I was no longer in love and finding it increasingly difficult to live with the person I had married. I seemed to make it all so complicated—and just by being silent. Being silent was so dangerous. So debilitating. It seemed so harmless, but some poison seemed harmless, too. Or acid, eating away at life itself. Sometimes it is good, but when one is in relationship with another being, it is not good. It is destructive. I felt very sad. Sad about the way I was inside. Sad to be contracted. Sad to cut myself off from life. Sad to affect my wife so harshly. Sad to see and not act. Sad to be sad.

Finally, with the help of my therapist, I did open up and speak, *but my wife didn't want to hear. She refused to enter marital counseling, as I requested, although I, too, had little hope it would help. Seeing that the prognosis was poor, I left the house and marriage in July, 1988, sputtering some in a muck of guilt and doubt in the few weeks before that.*

*Through it all, I walked and watched, and—yes—cried. Feeling the pulse of nature with my body connected my spirit to a part of the universe that never died—to a part of the universe the coyote knew—at deep, deep levels of understanding. Seeing coyotes, often close to the city, and reflecting on the wildness and resilience they symbolized, helped me through this damn difficult time.*

The first time our eyes met, I froze, and so did the coyote. The meeting happened on a ridge above Berkeley, mid-morning, November, the kind of day that had lured me from the dull, numb Novembers of New Hampshire. I was shocked at first, not at sighting this animal but that we were so close. The coyote stood higher up, on a rocky rise above the trail, and after about fifteen seconds, which seemed like an hour, this predator, whose call symbolized the West, turned and trotted upward and out of sight. My breathing took a heave and continued. So did the memory. I had seen my first coyote in the wild.

A young one, I thought, not so wary of human beings. Two hundred years of being tracked, poisoned, and shot, and the coyote still had a soft edge to the eyes, an unhurriedness to the gait. Was the animal injured, or just unafraid? No, not injured, I reckoned. Tilden Regional Park offered protection. No guns allowed. No angry ranchers. No pelt hunters. No bounties. A coyote could feel at home.

And this was truly Coyote's home. No need for a deed, no

building permits, no assessor. Coyote just lived a simple life, hunting what was available, taking nothing except to survive. Not a trickster, not a varmint, not a scurrilous predator, as often branded, but just Coyote, doing what coyotes have done long before humans arrived.

I saw the coyote again—I'm sure it was the same animal—at another time near the same spot on the Sea View Trail, the one that looped off the Big Springs Trail and climbed to heaven. Wide and multi-use (as the recreation technicians referred to it), it was part of the East Bay Skyline National Trail, and its views took in just about everything in four counties.

I saw the coyote near the crest, near the circle of stone that some say is an Indian power spot. Power spot or not, it commanded a 360-degree view, including Mount Diablo, Mount Tamalpais, almost all of San Francisco, four bay bridges, and, at certain magical moments, twilight extravaganzas featuring a setting sun over the Marin hills and a rising moon over Diablo, bathed in an alpenglow sunset sky. At times, lurching tentacles of fog reached over the ridge for Contra Costa County but not quite making it down to San Pablo Reservoir.

This day started clear, windy, clean as ice but warmer. Morning set the pace, and the coyote gamboled down just in front of the power spot. This time I followed, finally not forgetting my camera when it was most needed. The wild being stayed enough ahead to remind me that it was a wild being. On this day, that wildness involved stalking and hunting some small animal and waltzing through high grass and standing on rocks looking around. Keeping low on my belly, I crept like a lizard, moving only when the coyote moved. I knew I'd been noticed, though . . . and tolerated as long as I stayed outside a certain instinctive boundary. Surprised by the trusting nature of this wild animal, I inched closer than I'd expected to get and gave thanks to be permitted entry into this field of dreams.

In this time our worlds overlapped. Trust and simplicity must be tempered with wariness and strategy. A road, something convenient and straightforward to me, posed a problem to Coyote, who had to appraise and judge it in the course of daily events—much different from wild places that didn't as often require such an adjustment.

A human analogy would be the collapse of a bridge or the loss of a major road to repairs, forcing our migration/commuting patterns to change. South Park Drive, a road that bisected previously-wild Tilden Park, represented the same challenge to Coyote, only *Canis latrans's* biological clock, so linked to ours, might be ticking faster. Its life and well-being depended on territory, and Coyote's was shrinking rapidly.

Mountain bikes, too, a source of recreation and fun in my world, were a source of danger in Coyote's. Airplanes, electric fences, dogs, and even talking people were commonplace in my world. But in Coyote's world, strategic moves had to be made. What seemed safe in the morning might now be impassable. A detour might be needed, or a place to lie low for awhile, letting stillness and silence dissolve the intruder with a lack of interest.

This human-created world must appear strange and frightening to wild beings. They have the same kind of nerve endings and gray matter as we, and their senses were even more sensitized from continual use. I respected wild animals because they worked at their freedom. They had to. Yet Coyote's freedom had been crimped, its movements more restricted. Wary eyes scanned more, for the un-expected, for the twist within territory that was once, long, long ago, more trustworthy. Coyote has made accommodations and, much more so than man, has been The Great Compromiser.

And what Coyote has had to compromise is a part of being wild. Yet compromise seems not to be a problem. Coyote has adapted well to people. Unlike cougars, or kit foxes, or bears, Coyote has learned to live on the perimeter of our society, and, indeed, although many people would not be willing to admit it, Coyote has remained a part of our society—part of our vernacular landscape.

That the coyote I saw is on the run in the Tilden hills is a manifestation of human use of that formerly wild landscape. But like other species under stress from the man-made, Coyote is a reminder—a powerful reminder of spirit, free and wild. Coyote is a reminder that survival, and even growth, needn't have certainty for a base. Courage is what's needed, and the wisdom to stay out of harm's way.

I have not seen the coyote in Tilden for quite some time now, and to keep my own wildness alive I needed the actual experience of seeing. My social conditioning was too strong to use only visualization. I feared this wild being might have retreated to more remote and distant grounds. A woman was murdered in Tilden Park last year, and another was raped, and a man was seen walking naked on a trail near Inspiration Point. I wondered if the coyote's nerve endings sensed the increased human violence and insensitivity and opted for one more adjustment: that of leaving altogether. Even I, a much-less-sensitive being, avoided this wonderful park as a result of the violence.

I looked up at the photograph I took of the coyote. The photo seemed to come alive and the animal to move. In the high grass, full, rusty fur lightened darker eucalyptus in the background. The coyote played and pounced, unconcerned. Would our world keep pushing away instead of protecting? Would our world continue to destroy *our* world?

We are so linked, Coyote and I. Yet *my* wild nature lay hidden within—hidden beneath the mail of socialization. I roam the hills, hoping to find it. I light the fireplace on hot summer nights. I backpack and camp out. I eat raw foods. It is not enough. I need Coyote . . . to remember. No, I have not seen Coyote in the Tilden Hills for a long time, and I feel a little lost.

The Sea View Trail continued beyond the power spot, with its bench and picnic table like thrones above Valhalla, high above the frequent fog line—fog that filled the East Bay bowl like chilled whipped cream. Up here, though, the sun shone more than below, and the land hosted soaring Red-tailed Hawks and trusting California newts and plodding darkling "stink" beetles and speedy Western fence lizards . . . and, after you forked right, off the Sea View back onto the other end of the Big Springs, a couple of Great Horned Owls—if you were lucky . . . and quiet—silhouetted on the evening sky, conversing while perched in pine trees.

The trail wound back down to the parking lot, encouraging the kind of walking that forced the arms into a free swing. Resistance to my swinging arms fell away, and for a moment wildness emerged with the swinging and wind in the hair. Somewhere in the hills above or beyond, Coyote burrowed into a den—to care for pups or eat prey or remember the day and howl both a requiem and refrain in a rhapsody of survival.

(Last year, the United States Department of Agriculture killed almost 96,000 coyotes to protect livestock—as they call other animals—and yet this wild predator continues to survive as a species in our land.)

 ANT WARS

The end of marriage did not, unfortunately, bring stress-free simplicity to life in the city. But I was, by and large, happier living alone. With the cancer book job over, my struggle to earn a freelance livelihood in one of the more expensive urban areas in the country continued anew. But I sold a book proposal of essays about walks and the history of the Bay Area to a Santa Cruz publisher and got a small advance, and that, with income from articles and nursing-home musical performances, allowed me to finish the book, which did well enough so that the publisher agreed to a sequel the following year.

To save money I cut my overhead by moving to a reasonably safe, and cheap, in-law unit in the hills above drug-infested East Oakland and soon discovered that the landlord was a jazz trumpet player and the ceiling was made of cardboard. Not exactly a quiet enclave. But without the business of marriage to run, I did some quality writing there.

*My body became healthier, too, because I now found more time to hike; my spirit brightened as I saw a potentially positive future instead of a feeling I was dying imminently; and my mind became more peaceful, helping me deal with the unexpected and unwanted, like ants.*

They have finally left. Not that I had anything to do with it. No, their leaving was completely an internal decision, coming directly from their own Politburo. For the last few days their strategy was a simple one: take over territory previously held by their ancestors but only recently—about ten thousand years ago—homesteaded by the two-legged ones.

During those few days, they convoyed massive numbers of troops unreported in the two-legged press but covered thoroughly in the ant-disestablishment press (the "dis" meaning "disassemble the"). Ants completely overwhelmed defensive positions in a south cupboard, securing the famed Honey Hill. In fact, the battle for Honey Hill was so intense that a monument was constructed there, and subsequent generations—there have been several since the battle two days ago—come back for pilgrimages, pointing out to their offspring where their great-grandfathers died and the spot where Ole Five-legged Jim led the final triumphant charge up Sugar Frosted Ridge.

Once the cupboard was secured, ant commanders focused their antennae on the desk of the two-legged trespasser. They ordered scouts to reconnoiter the cluttered north flank, the place filled with long-windowed envelopes and what seemed like thousands of papers—totally useless papers in the context of actual survival. They found nothing sweet or sticky or crumbly, but their preliminary reports must have indicated something of interest because more came, exploring the crevices of computer, printer, calculator, phone, and its answering companion that seemed to always speak of not being home, and exploring, ultimately, even the two-legged one—the starer out of windows, the opener of refrigerator doors, the drinker of tea, the eater of corn on the cob. Yes, at times the eater—that's me—would occasionally leave dishes on the vast, cluttered desk, and ant platoons mapped out every conceivable approach to them.

With desk sentries well entrenched, commanders skilled in the art of psychological warfare zeroed in on what they knew was the ultimate bastion of the two-legged one's security, the place that, if penetrated, could drive out the curmudgeon. Topographical maps showed it to be a large plateau, not unlike a high chaparral, soft to the touch, whose terrain changed constantly. It proved to be the bed of the two-legged one, and the ant commanders knew from prior campaigns what kind of disgust they could arouse by sending troops into that theater.

Up to this time they were quite surprised to find that the human inhabitant resorted not to killing the troops but to scooping them up and putting them back on a window sill or even at times outside. Their intelligence teams ran a background check and found the two-legged one was a one-time Buddhist who often struggled with existential issues of life. Lately, though, he had left the Middle Way to follow the teachings of a non-physical channeled entity who advocated having fun and creating success. This change alarmed the commanders, for obviously the two-legged one would not consider sharing his space with ants as the pinnacle of fun and success. Quite the contrary, they reasoned. And after a thorough analysis of the New Age entity's ideas (cadres had infiltrated his South Palm Beach, Florida, offices and ant-faxed the info), commanders concluded the entity was specie-ist in nature, finding no canons not to kill.

The Battle of the Bed, an out-and-out bloodbath, finally pushed the two-legged one—that's me—over the edge of oneness with all things into the pit of alienation, anomie, and blatant violence. Ant history books depict the brave deeds of soldiers who climbed the steep crags of Pillow Heights to get to the head of the beast and of saboteurs who trekked inches over the Cover Steppes to actually ascend the body of the two-legged one in a valiant effort to awaken him in the middle of the night, thus driving a wedge between him and sane consciousness. If he wanted a New Age, they'd show him a New Age, one in which ants assume their rightful place on the planet and, eventually, the entire universe.

What they didn't count on, though, was the depth of his ability to sleep through anything. They crawled on all sixes through the hair on his arms and legs, got on his vulnerable neck, and even conquered, with small ropes and pitons purchased at the well-known cooperative outdoor equipment store, REAnts, the crevices of his face—all to no avail. He would not awaken. And in the morning he methodically picked up and squashed, between huge pincer-like fingers, the brave and tired ant warriors.

At this time, too, intelligence picked up coded messages from the two-legged one to someone he referred to as the landlord, although decoders fouled up a bit and translated it as warlord. The mistake was fitting, for in short order, four divisions were wiped out by a poison gas attack perpetrated by this fearsome warlord on outside escarpments. What's more, the two-legged one started a campaign of spraying ammonia, in the form of common glass cleaner, on all ant supply lines, killing hundreds immediately. (Ammonia is to ants as kryptonite is to Superman.)

With battles raging on at least four different fronts, commanders of all units met at a now-historic meeting not far from Honey Hill and agreed to a strategy, called G-Day, the G signifying *Garbage*. All divisions advanced west, past Old Sink Canyon, to the Tasty Wastelands, where began a massive operation to salvage food and war materials to support the ravaged troops. Again, they knew how disgusting this would be to the two-legged one and were hoping he would pull out when confronted with awesome numbers, particularly when he would bring into the territory another two-legged one of the female sex. Ant psychologists had done extensive studies of the effect of previous campaigns on the ego structure of two-legged ones and particularly the way the campaigns affected the relationships between these beings. They had documented cases in which extended families of two-legged ones were broken apart and demoralized by the incessant heroics of ant armies.

This time, though, the strategy failed, as day after day the two-legged one took small bags of garbage to outside cans. The ants couldn't secure the Tasty Wastelands. And soon the entire crusade came to a halt.

So they finally left, for the time being. An occasional soldier could still be seen carrying a dead comrade back to who-knows-where, but the vast armies vanished.

An uneasy calm descended over the territories I called my apartment. Were they repopulating? Were they planning for the next incursion? Were they evolving strains of super-ants, impervious to ammonia and Bendiocarb: 2.2-dimethyl-1,3-benzodioxol-4-ol methylcarbamate? I sat there among the carcasses and war monuments, gazed out the window for a long while, went to the refrigerator, put a plate of food on my desk, and wondered who was watching from nearby trenches.

# FALLING FREE

In October of 1990 I marked my forty-fifth birthday. I could not report having accumulated great wealth ... or fame ... or family. But I had managed to stay in relatively good shape, given the meat grinder the last few years had felt like. "I feel a muted sadness," I wrote in my journal shortly after my Halloween birthday. "A lilting laughter, an ache in my back. I am alone. Yet I am not lonely. I am alive. I am alive. I am a writer, and I am alive."

I began teaching writing and liked it, as did my students. I began dating, like a normal middle-aged single man (I know that's replete with oxymorons!), without having to fall in love every two months, and to remind myself I wrote a song called "Take it Slow." I meditated on the origins of thought, a meditation prompting me to write, " ... when I don't think, I am happy. One runaway thought, though, and I'm in a spin. Can I not leave my self alone? Must I always get in the way of *peace of mind? Tears come, without thought, without contrivance, without fear. Life really is simple . . . as long as I don't figure it out."*

I walked my spirit trail often, consulting an inner guide on life on this physical plane. I listened closely, but the nature of my own life was still plagued by seemingly karmic money woes and their accompanying anxiety. So I did the only viable thing one can do in a situation like that: pieced my resumé together and applied for and got a good-paying part-time job working with mentally disabled people, something I had done for many years before concentrating on writing.

This job became more than a way of making money, though, as these people I worked with increasingly inched their way into my heart and taught me something of courage in the face of the horrendous realities of a schizophrenic break and society's often archaic responses of ostracism and ignorance. They taught me something of falling, when emotional ground suddenly gave way; and of fear, when the physical body/mind remembered and anticipated its happening again; and of freedom, when the spirit self felt the fear but acted anyway.

The night before my friend and I fell off a cliff at Point Reyes National Seashore, I was telling a fellow Christmas party reveler that walking had never caused me any problems. On the contrary, I told him, walking had always provided a clarity of mind that helped me to solve problems and at times to navigate through some pretty murky waters.

Perhaps it was a mistake to tempt fate like that, for the following day a female friend and I set out—it was our first date—on an eight-mile jaunt to a lovely place called Alamere Falls, a wonderland where water fell pell-mell from a high cliff onto the beach. And for seven of those miles, all was well. We talked and walked and sat and picnicked and laughed and even kissed and hugged.

*STEPHEN ALTSCHULER*

But in the eighth mile we saw first-hand proof of the Buddha's admonition that life can change as quickly as the swish of a horse's tail. We started back from the falls late—around four—with darkness gradually, almost imperceptibly, overtaking the light. We were both feeling buoyant from the falls, the ocean, the sounds, the pelicans, the warm California winter sun. I had a flashlight in my fanny pack but was liking the sensing of the trail with my feet.

"You know, I used to cross-country ski in New Hampshire at night without a light, and I did my best skiing then," I told her, remembering the exhilarating feeling of plummeting down an incline using my feet, my gut, my heart, but not my eyes to reach the bottom. At those times I had no fear and never skied better. "It is getting pretty dark, though. Would you like a light?"

"No," she answered. "I kind of like this feeling of walking in the dark." She must have been a little scared, I thought. But I let it go and continued talking animatedly about dark New Hampshire nights.

"I had to walk about a mile through the woods to my place there and. . . ." The next word I do not remember, for it never came out. Instead, I dropped from the seemingly solid trail into an abyss that ended about fifteen feet down, although at the time I couldn't tell how far down I was.

In the next instant, something came tumbling down on top of me—a rock, I thought, from the crumbling, unstable cliff bank. But a rock does not groan. It was my date, and she was a few feet below me, having tried to grab me as I fell and getting too close herself to the gravelly edge. Her wrist was broken, and I mean broken, shaped now like a lightning bolt. My ankle was sore, but I knew intuitively it was intact.

In one false step—literally, a step—life had changed and would never be quite the same. There would now be memory—memory of falling, memory of losing ground, memory of the danger of walking at night near a cliff without a light. The fall itself took less than a second, but within that time the seed of a lifetime was planted.

I would respect the night more now. I would be more careful of knowing the terrain at any given point. I would anticipate more, not out of fear but out of the memory of experience. I would pay more attention to the act of walking itself instead of being intoxicated with talk, leaving walking to fend for itself. Walking needed attention. Walking needed care. Walking needed love.

I would remember, too, falling—a state human beings are unaccustomed to. It has been a long time since we swung from tree to tree, falling in between until we could grab another vine. It has been a long time since we jumped off a cliff into a deep lagoon of clear blue water. We try, at all cost, to avoid falling. We insure ourselves against it. We safeguard our bathrooms. We shovel and chisel and salt our sidewalks to make sure it doesn't happen. We equate falling with disaster: airplanes crashing; people on thin ice; a collapsing section of the Bay Bridge and portion of a freeway interchange after the big 1989 quake in the Bay Area. Entire movies are based on the fear and anticipation of falling. The word evokes images of broken bones, emergency wards, casts, and sometimes death.

But when I fell, I was unafraid. If a stop-action camera had filmed my face during the fall, it would have recorded no panic. I think, instead, that my face must have been quite serene, somehow comfortable with falling, enjoying the feeling of space around me with nothing solid to inhibit or constrict. It wasn't the falling that presented the problem as much as the ground I hit when the fall stopped and the ground I looked up at as I pondered our predicament.

Later, the experience made me wonder if death was like falling and birth was the ground we eventually hit. I'd always been afraid of the idea of death as well as the idea of falling, but the feeling of falling itself was enlivening. When I was airborne no problem existed. Could death, too, be exhilarating—a kind of falling with no surrounding ground? Could birth be the ground that suddenly, rudely, intrudes on the ecstatic falling of death?

*STEPHEN ALTSCHULER*

After the fall, lighting the way with the previously-shunned flashlight I hauled myself out of the dark abyss. Then I hoisted my injured new friend out, pulling her arm so straight that in the process I cured a trick elbow of hers. Her wrist was obviously fractured, although I tried valiantly to wish it otherwise. Thankfully, she was not in much pain. My ankle hurt, but we could both trek the remaining mile back to the trailhead. We were lucky, I guessed. The drop to the ocean near that point was at least 200 feet.

Yet during that second in the air, from the trail to the ledge below, maybe I *was* in a state of death, in a state of falling, and, without the mind to deny it, or explain it, or worry about it, or lament it, I was free. At peace.

No, I don't recommend taking a dive off a cliff. But maybe the mind doesn't always have to have a ground, a reason for everything, a need for tangible reassurance. Maybe I can let myself fly a little more, take more risks, and even fall. It's a thought that's scary but somehow exciting and life-affirming.

Of course, these musings were all well and good, but when my friend Bob asked me the day after the fall what lesson the universe was trying to teach me, what came to mind was (1) use a light when hiking at night, and (2) on a first date, go to a movie.

# EPILOGUE

The city to the country to the city to the country-within-the-city: I have been almost fifteen years looking for a balance of inner landscape with outer, a balance of making a living with actually living, of idealism with pragmatism, of magic with the mundane, of preference with need, of spirituality with reality, of the uncertainty of life with the certainty of death. I have sought community in those years, at times solely with trees and creeks and woodchucks, at times in marriage, at times with friends and neighbors, all the time trying to integrate and unify the community within myself—

to attune disparate parts and emotions and attempt to create inner harmony, peace, and happiness.

Place—where I live and the situation I live in—is integral to that search for balance. Place is a mirror telling me where the pendulum swinging in my soul is at any given time. This is not to say that one place is better than another, but one place, and my level of settledness there, may be more favorable to personal growth than another. Asking "Is this where I want ultimately to be?" tells me if I'm there out of preference or need, love or expediency, livelihood or leisure.

Questions like that, along with Who am I? and What if I had only six more months to live? and What do I want? and What is this life all about? propel each external migration, which in turn fuels each internal movement. And it is the seemingly opposite nature of the places I've lived in that sets up a kind of internal electromagnetic force field—a field where positive and negative charges attract each other to generate energy that powers me forward. This field could be a conflict of opposites, as C. G. Jung referred to it, and it feels like a conflict at times, but when I look back it is just as much a play of opposites—like digging a root cellar, struggling with inner and outer forces, thus leading me to see a resilient, determined side of myself that served me well through the rest of the years at the cabin; and falling, after moving to the city, twice suffering injury, thus spurring me to observe life in a new light and lifting me a little further out of the pit of ignorance; and living within the noise, commotion, and danger of the city, thus making me more aware of the quiet places, the country within the city, the small acts of courtesy, friendliness, and compassion that nurture and heal my spirit.

Even the wrenching experiences of the suicide of an ex-spouse and divorce from a second wife created openings my heart had hitherto avoided. I had to look within. I had to look at my relationship to life and living. The pain prodded me to look, and what

I saw drove me to examine my own patterns, feelings, doubts, values, capacities, and abilities to adapt to change.

Adapting to the changes of life: perhaps that is what I learned most over these years. From the harsh exigencies of a north-woods cabin, to the unexpected loss of someone I had been intimate with, to city life that felt overwhelming at times, to a second gut-wrenching divorce, I've come to realize, through watching the moments closely and judging them less and less, that change is a basic truth. And I've come to realize that I can use that truth to walk the wire between taking things too lightly and taking things too seriously. Through accepting change I can be more at peace with change in whatever form.

I see, too, that the universe breathes a common breath—that every thing alive breathes and feels fear when that breath is threatened and safety when that breath is secure. By keeping my senses open I feel more connected to all around me, including those I see suffering on the evening news half-way around the world. I see that the community I am seeking, therefore, encompasses other worlds besides my front and back yards. I can affect and am affected by events happening anywhere.

Since the completion of this book I have moved again: this time back to the country, this time to a middle ground between the primitive cabin and the city apartment. I don't know if this is my final destination, but because of the emotional and spiritual ground I've tilled over these years I feel more ready than ever to sink my boots into the mud of this place and slip and slide and fall as I may. I feel more prepared to die, not physically, but to each moment as I mud-walk along, living with all the skill and awareness possible— living "happily ever insecure."